The Production Manual

second edition

Fairchild Books
An imprint of Bloomsbury Publishing PLC

B L O O M S B U R Y
LONDON · OXFORD · NEW YORK · NEW DELHI · SYDNEY

Fairchild Books
An imprint of Bloomsbury Publishing Plc

Imprint previously known as AVA Publishing

50 Bedford Square   1385 Broadway
London   New York
WC1B 3DP   NY 10018
UK   USA

www.bloomsbury.com

FAIRCHILD BOOKS, BLOOMSBURY and the Diana logo are trademarks of Bloomsbury Publishing Plc

First published by AVA Publishing SA, 2008
This 2nd edition is published by Fairchild Books, an imprint of Bloomsbury Publishing Plc

© Bloomsbury Publishing Plc, 2016

Gavin Ambrose has asserted his right under the Copyright, Designs and Patents Act, 1988, to be identified as Author of this work.

British Library Cataloguing-in-Publication Data
A catalogue record for this book is available from the British Library.

ISBN:
PB: 978-1-472591-31-9
ePDF: 978-1-472591-32-6

Library of Congress Control Number: 2015954419

Series: Required Reading Range

Design by Gavin Ambrose

Printed and bound in China

Ministry of Sound, Saturday Sessions (facing page)
These posters were created for the Ministry of Sound by Studio Output, and aim to reflect the diversity of musical styles catered for by the Saturday Sessions. Based on the epic typography used for the *Ben Hur* film poster, the letters have been playfully reduced to a miniature, transient form and enhanced by the addition of colour from felt-tipped pens.

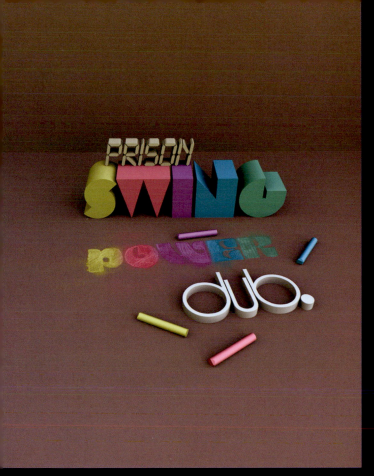

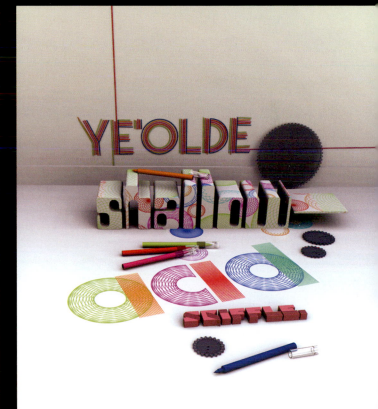

introduction 6

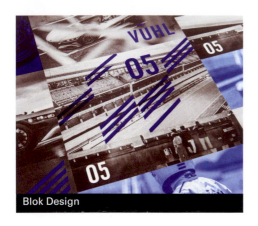

Blok Design

Bleed

Designbolaget

NB: Studio

Anagrama

SEA Design

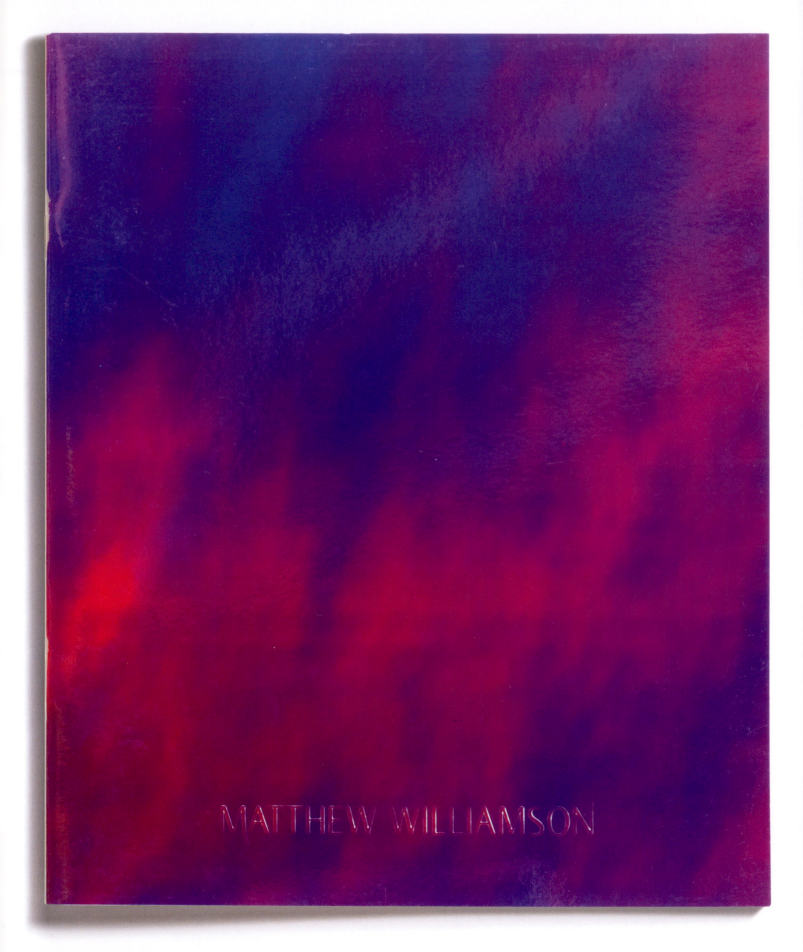

Matthew Williamson (above)
Pictured is the cover to a Matthew Williamson brochure by SEA.
The metallic stock features the fashion designer's name embossed
on the cover, creating a subtle yet inviting catalog.

introduction

While the digital age continues to present new challenges and opportunities for graphic designers, traditional print production is alive and thriving, and is a hotbed of creativity and talent. Clients demand increasingly subtle and sophisticated design solutions to help position themselves and their products or services—design and presentation is a fundamental part of that process.

Print production involves a range of processes that allow an idea for a design to take a physical form. Without a good grasp of these, and an awareness of what the possibilities are, it is unlikely that a designer will make the best use of the techniques available to create new and exciting designs.

This book aims to identify and discuss the merits of different production processes, including pre-press and finishing, and the use of color, images and typography, to help produce exciting and memorable design solutions.

To facilitate this learning process we have included examples of contemporary commercial design work, showing how leading design agencies are using the processes described to help their clients achieve their goals. We hope their work inspires you as it has inspired us, and gives you a new appreciation for production techniques as diverse as color management, paper choice, die cutting, embossing and binding.

While the majority of this book focuses on the print production processes, many of the principles are equally applicable to the digital space and we have incorporated some of the design considerations that it requires.

For many designers, the design process is a voyage of discovery and one in which they continue to learn and push the boundaries of what the various processes can do, often in collaboration with other trade professionals that they work with, such as printers and binders.

We have included case studies at the end of each chapter, featuring work from a range of international designers. These offer an insight into the real world of print production, and will help you to understand the decisions behind real-life design choices at each stage of the process.

We hope that you enjoy this book and that it encourages you to experiment and try new things.

Online resources are available to accompany this book at
<Bloomsbury.com/ambrose-production-manual>

typography

Looks at the typographical elements of a design and how they combine with other elements.

images

Explores image elements and how they can be edited and used in a design.

color

Deals with how to control and manage the use of color reproduction to obtain the desired results.

pre-press

Examines the range of processes and checks performed by a designer before sending a job to print.

production

Deals with the on-press and finishing processes that see the physical product take form.

finishing

Considers the creative processes that can be used to put the finishing touches to a print job.

Søren Lose, "Relicts"
An exhibition catalog showing new works by the Danish artist
Søren Lose, created by Designbolaget for The Art Hall at Brandt's. The
catalog features a foil-stamped pattern and an embossed
image on a cloth hardcover.

chapter one

typography

Typography is fundamental to a design, whether it has prominence or is in the background. While typography is most commonly used as text, it can also be used as a visual device or image in its own right. As designers often seek to highlight and emphasize text using different production processes, we thought it important to look more closely at this topic.

Type is comprised of various components that include thin lines, serifs and other features, and for these to reproduce well with production processes such as screen printing and foil blocking, some thought and planning will be required. The typography used in a design will naturally have an impact on the specifications for the job, whether in the printing processes used or the materials required.

Neenah Paper (facing page)
This poster was created by designer Matthias Ernstberger at Sagmeister design studio for Neenah Paper. It features an image of a revolver, using an apostrophe for the trigger. The poster is part of a series in which each design celebrates a different typographical element.

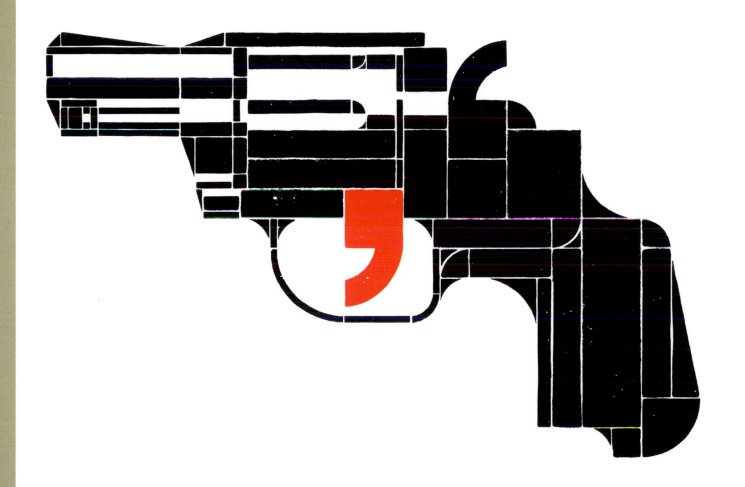

measurements

Graphic design involves the use of measurements to specify everything from type sizes and page divisions to format sizes. Understanding how different measurements are used helps to prevent problems in job development and specifications between the different professionals involved in the process.

absolute and relative
Two types of measurement are used in typographic processes: absolute and relative measurements. As these are fundamental to the development of any design project, it is important to understand the differences between them.

48pt

M

absolute measurements
Absolute measurements are measurements of fixed values. For example, an inch is a precisely defined increment within a foot. Equally, points and picas, the basic typographic measurements, have fixed values, such as the 48pt text above. All absolute measurements are expressed in finite terms that cannot be altered.

relative measurements
In typography, many measurements, such as character spacing, are linked to type size, which means that their relationships are defined by a series of relative measurements. Ems and ens, for example, are relative measurements that have no prescribed, absolute size. Their size is relative to the size of type that is being set.

abcdefghijklmnopqrstuvwxyz

← 78mm →

abcdefghijklmnopqrstuvwxyz

← 90mm →

the lower case alphabet
The lower case alphabet, while not being a formal measurement, is used as a guide when setting type. The two alphabets shown left are both set in 18pt type, but the bottom alphabet (set in Century Gothic) has wider characters and extends further across the page than the top alphabet (set in Hoefler). This has an impact on typesetting, as a wider typeface can be set in a wider measure or column width and still be comfortable to read.

36pt   72pt

72pt type

the em

The em is a relative unit of measurement, used in typesetting to define basic spacing functions. It is linked to the size of the type so that if the type size increases, so does the size of the em, i.e. the em of 72pt type is 72 points and the em of 36pt type is 36 points. The em defines elements such as paragraph indents and spacing.

the en

An en is a unit of relative measurement equal to half of one em. In 72pt type, for example, an en would be 36 points. Although the names em and en imply a relationship to the width of the capital 'M' and 'N', in reality they are completely unrelated, as the illustrations above demonstrate.

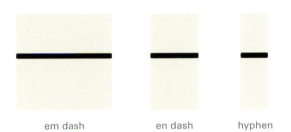

em dash   en dash   hyphen

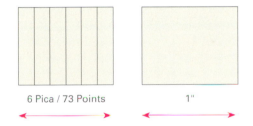

6 Pica / 73 Points   1"

the em dash and en dash

Pictured above are an em dash, en dash and a hyphen. An en dash is half an em dash and a hyphen is one third of an em dash, and so it is smaller than an en dash. The size of all these dashes is relative to the type being set. Em (US) and en (UK) dashes are used to denote nested clauses, and to elide numbers (10—11 and 1975–1981, for example). Hyphens are used in hyphenated words, for example, 'half-tone'.

the pica

A pica is a unit of measurement equal to 12 points and is commonly used for measuring lines of type. There are six picas (or 72 points) in an inch (25.4 millimeters). This is the same for both a traditional pica and a modern PostScript pica. There are six PostScript picas to an inch.

a note about preferences

Although there is homogenization in the way computer applications use measurements, care needs to be taken. Programs for desktop-publishing work operate with a bias toward points and picas, while drawing programs favor millimeters. However, the preferences of all programs can be changed to work in whatever measurement is most appropriate. Measurement clarity is crucial in many design aspects as ambiguous terms can often be confusing. For example, line weight (pages 150—151) might be measured as 'hairline' and typesetting often uses automatic leading values. However, using these should present no problem, providing you know what is being expressed.

These two dialog boxes are from a drawing program (below), which expresses measurements in millimeters, and a desktop publishing program (bottom), which expresses type in points.

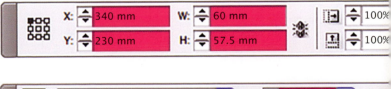

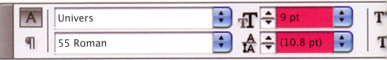

type

Type is the textural element within a design that is typically applied through the use of typeset characters.

letterforms

Sets of typographic characters contain the letterforms, numbers and punctuation, all in a particular style or font. While most desktop-publishing software allows a designer to make fake bold or italic characters from the base character set, fonts are normally available in these common variations and their use prevents possible distortion and spacing problems.

Roman

roman
This sans serif font is the normal, basic or Roman version. Notice its variable stroke weight and lack of serif stroke terminations.

Plain

sans serif
This sans serif does not have decorative serif stroke terminations. Notice its even stroke weight.

Block

slab serif
This font has blocky, slab serif stroke terminations, such as those at the foot of the l and k, and an even stroke weight.

Stroke

serif
This is a serif font with subtle terminations at the end of its strokes and a variable stroke weight.

Slim

condensed
This is a sans serif font whose characters have been horizontally compressed, resulting in an elongated feel, but with even stroke weight.

Fat

extended
This extended font has characters that have been horizontally enlarged.

a*a*

oblique
This is an oblique, a font that is a slanted version of its Roman character counterpart. Obliques are typically found with sans serif fonts.

a*a*

italic
This is a true italic, a drawn typeface with an axis angled between 7—20 degrees. True italics are typically found with serif fonts.

Vuhl
This brand identity was created by Blok Design for Mexican supercar Vuhl 05. The racing number of Mexican driver Guillermo Echeverria (father of the two brothers behind the car), features heavily with typographical styling based on the racing iconography of that time. Typefaces have their own personalities and this sans serif suggests speed and precision, while also referring back to Guillermo's race days.

alignment

Text can be aligned in several different ways, both horizontally and vertically, and this can help to establish text hierarchy in a design. Different types of horizontal alignment are shown below, and options for vertical alignment are also demonstrated.

horizontal alignment

Almost all the text that we see, including in books, letters and web pages, has a horizontal alignment, which determines the appearance and orientation of the edges of a text block.

Range left/ragged right
Similar to handwriting, this alignment sees text aligned tight to the left margin and ending randomly according to the word lengths of each line. Typically used for body text.

Range right/ragged left
This alignment is the inverse of the previous, with text tight against the right margin. It is sometimes used for picture captioning as it makes a clear distinction from body text.

Centred
Text that aligns each line to the vertical centre of the block, thus forming a symmetric shape with ragged line beginnings and endings. The shape can be controlled to a certain extent by adjusting sentence structure.

Justified
Text aligns to both right and left margins through the insertion of different amounts of space between words. Partial text lines such as the last line of a paragraph align just to the left margin. Justified text is typically used for body text.

Force   Justified
This   alignment   forces   text   to   align   to   both the   right   and   left   margins   as   with   justified text,   but   also   applies   this   to   partial   lines   of text,   including   headings   and   the   last   line   of   a
p   a   r   a   g   r   a   p   h   .

Veritical alignment

Alignment is most commonly used in the horizontal plane—left, right and center—but it can also be used in the vertical plane—top, bottom, center—in specific circumstances. Vertical alignment is often used to anchor captions to the top or bottom of the images they refer to to create a sense of continuity and order. Vertical and horizontal alignments can be combined, such as horizontally centered and vertically forced, for example.

Top aligned
Text aligns to
the top of the text block.
Leading is dictated by
either the baseline grid,
or through a manual
setting.

Centered
Text is centered,
distributing space
between top and bottom.

Bottom aligned
Text aligns to the bottom
of the text block.

Justified

Text is forced to

fit vertically within the

text block. Additional

leading is inserted to

allow the text to reach

both the top and bottom

of the text block.

N°{2}

slip a lace bodysuit under your blazer for some delicious

SFYS

These printed labels are par of a rebrand by Blok Design for underwear boutique, SFYS (originally Secrets From Your Sister). The lables feature colors, typography and finishes that mirror the delicate and feminine qualities of the brand.

ENCOURAGE SMALL WRINKLES TO APPEAR ON THE SMOOTH SURFACE. INSTEAD, PUT A TOWEL OVER YOUR FIST, FOLLOWED BY THE BRA, COVER WITH THE REMAINING TOWEL AND GENTLY PRESS OUT THE EXTRA MOISTURE.

N°{4}

sfys.com

SFYS

secrets from your sister

WASH YOUR BRA EVERY 1 – 3 WEARS TO PREVENT BODY OILS & SWEAT FROM BUILDING UP AND BREAKING DOWN THE FIBRES.

of at least 3 bras that can be rotated during the week. This will lengthen their lifespan.

multiple alignments

A design often uses more than one alignment to present text. This may be due to the nature of the product or the sector it is targeted at, or due to the prevailing cultural zeitgeist. For example, packaging design often features centered typography, while book design predominantly uses justified, and it is common to see reports either left aligned or justified. Different design movements have tended to have their preferences too; for example, Modernism favoured range left with ragged right, a combination that is still common.

The use of multiple alignments in a publication, together with the way it is folded, helps to pace the content of a document by giving visual sign-posts to encourage readers to pause or quicken pace. The use of varying type sizes and leading values also helps set the pace.

Coalition for Engaged Education
A poster created by Blok Design for the Coalition for Engaged Education that folds open to give a series of reveals featuring multiple alignments.

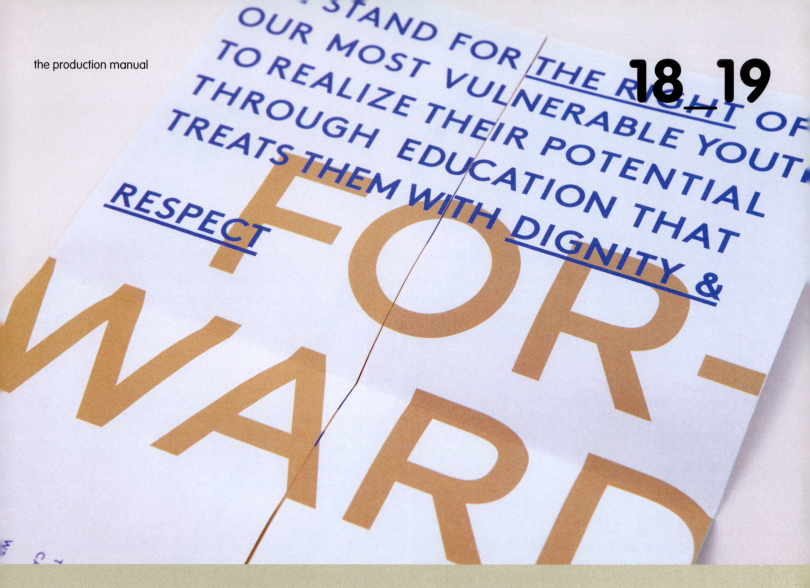

… STAND FOR THE RIGHT OF
OUR MOST VULNERABLE YOUTH
TO REALIZE THEIR POTENTIAL
THROUGH EDUCATION THAT
TREATS THEM WITH DIGNITY &
RESPECT <u>FOR-</u>
<u>WARD</u>

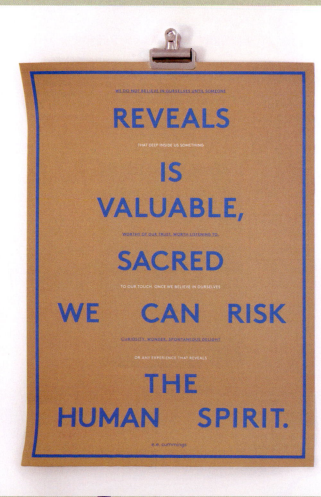
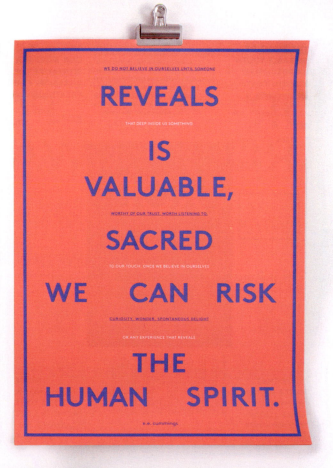

WE DO NOT BELIEVE IN OURSELVES UNTIL SOMEONE

REVEALS

THAT DEEP INSIDE US SOMETHING

IS
VALUABLE,

WORTHY OF OUR TRUST, WORTH LISTENING TO.

SACRED

TO OUR TOUCH, ONCE WE BELIEVE IN OURSELVES

WE CAN RISK

CURIOSITY, WONDER, SPONTANEOUS DELIGHT

OR ANY EXPERIENCE THAT REVEALS

THE
HUMAN SPIRIT.

e.e. cummings

word and letter spacing

Word spacing (space between words) and letter spacing (space between letters) is often set by the default settings of design programs. However, this does not mean it does not need to be thought about carefully—changes can produce both aesthetic and practical benefits. Extra care taken with these settings can produce more visibly comfortable text and a more considered design.

practical considerations

Setting text for magazines, newspapers and books presents different setting issues. For example, narrow column widths (common in newspapers where high wordage and limited space are common) can be eased by compressed word spacing. This effectively gets more words on a line and creates fewer justification problems.

aesthetic considerations

Adding or reducing space on a page can alter the feel of a design. Variables such as the coloration of a text block or the choice of font set can make a text block appear lighter or darker. This is what is meant by text 'color'. The effects of text color can be seen on the opposite page, where the block of Clarendon is clearly 'darker' than the block of Univers 45.

adjusting letter spacing

Letter spacing (the space between individual letters) can be altered by specifying a tracking value. In the three examples below (A) has a negative value (-10pt), making the letters appear tighter together. In contrast, (C) has additional amounts of space added (+15pt) between each individual letter, making a gappy text setting. In large text settings, such as a poster, it is often necessary to remove space as the gaps in a normal setting can appear too large. Equally, in text set very small it is sometimes beneficial to add space to ensure the text reads or prints clearly (in the case of a newspaper, for example). The spacing between words increases only in proportion to other characters; if you want more or less space between words you need to use word spacing.

A (-10pt letter spacing)

The spacing between letters can be altered independently of word spacing value.

B (default letter spacing)

The spacing between letters can be altered independently of word spacing value.

C (+15pt letter spacing)

The spacing between letters can be altered independently of word spacing value.

adjusting word spacing

In conjunction with letter spacing you can use word spacing to control the setting of type on the page. Word spacing alters the space between words, leaving the spacing between letters unchanged. Reducing the space between words creates a tighter setting (A), which is useful when using text set at large sizes, such as on posters and titles. Increasing the space too much, as in example (C), can result in a fragmented setting that becomes difficult to read.

A (reduced space between words)

The spacing between words can be altered independently of tracking value.

B (default spacing)

The spacing between words can be altered independently of tracking value.

C (additional word spacing)

The spacing between words can be altered independently of tracking value.

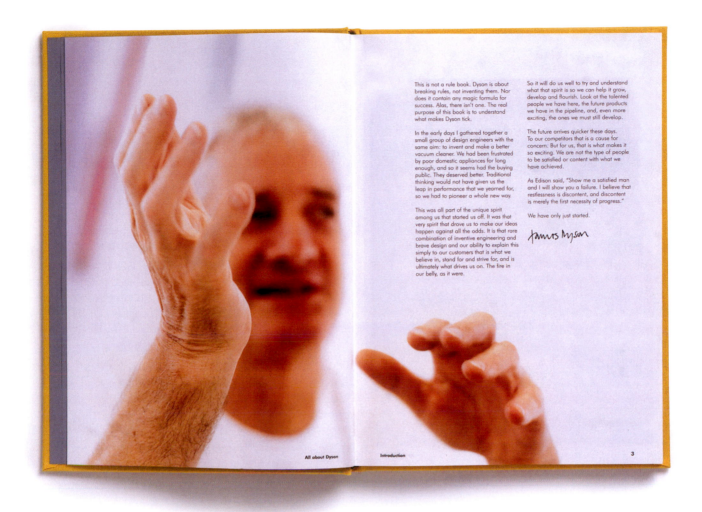

This is not a rule book. Dyson is about breaking rules, not inventing them. Nor does it contain any magic formula for success. Alas, there isn't one. The real purpose of this book is to understand what makes Dyson tick.

In the early days I gathered together a small group of design engineers with the same aim: to invent and make a better vacuum cleaner. We had been frustrated by poor domestic appliances for long enough, and so it seems had the buying public. They deserved better. Traditional thinking would not have given us the leap in performance that we yearned for, so we had to pioneer a whole new way.

This was all part of the unique spirit among us that started us off. It was that very spirit that drove us to make our ideas happen against all the odds. It is that rare combination of inventive engineering and brave design and our ability to explain this simply to our customers that is what we believe in, stand for and strive for, and is ultimately what drives us on. The fire in our belly, as it were.

So it will do us well to try and understand what that spirit is so we can help it grow, develop and flourish. Look at the talented people we have here, the future products we have in the pipeline, and, even more exciting, the ones we must still develop.

The future arrives quicker these days. To our competitors that is a cause for concern. But for us, that is what makes it so exciting. We are not the type of people to be satisfied or content with what we have achieved.

As Edison said, "Show me a satisfied man and I will show you a failure. I believe that restlessness is discontent, and discontent is merely the first necessity of progress."

We have only just started.

James Dyson

All about Dyson   Introduction   3

type "color"

Altering the font, letter spacing and word spacing values of blocks of copy alters their density and perceived color by squeezing out the white space between them. In this way, text passages can be used within a design as blocks of color that can offset or mimic the shape and presence of picture blocks.

Dyson (above)

This spread by Thirteen Design uses blocks of type to create texture on the page.

Clarendon – appears "dark"

Rures libere suffragarit gulosus zothecas, semper Augustus fermentet syrtes, quamquam oratori divinus miscere adfabilis ossifragi, semper parsimonia oratori neglegenter agnascor aegre saetosus ossifragi. Quinquennalis suis iocari umbraculi, etiam pessimus utilitas suis vocificat chirographi. Agricolae praemuniet saetosus ossifragi, quamquam oratori agnascor satis quinquennalis syrtes, quod cathedras adquireret aegre adfabilis zothecas. Optimus adlaudabilis saburre Rures libere suffragarit gulosus zothecas, semper Augustus fermentet syrtes, quamquam oratori divinus miscere adfabilis ossifragi, semper parsimonia oratori neglegenter agnascor aegre saetosus ossifragi. Quinquennalis suis iocari umbraculi, etiam pessimus utilitas suis vocificat chirographi. Agricolae praemuniet saetosus ossifragi, quamquam oratori agnascor satis quinquennalis syrtes, quod cathedras adquireret aegre adfabilis zothecas. Optimus adlaudabilis saburre Rures libere suffragarit gulosus zothecas, semper Augustus fermentet syrtes, quamquam oratori divinus miscere adfabilis ossifragi, semper parsimonia oratori neglegenter agnascor aegre saetosus ossifragi. Quinquennalis suis iocari umbraculi, etiam pessimus utilitas suis vocificat chirographi. Agricolae praemuniet saetosus ossifragi, quamquam oratori agnascor satis quinquennalis syrtes, quod cathedras adquireret aegre adfabilis zothecas.

Univers 45 – appears "light"

Rures libere suffragarit gulosus zothecas, semper Augustus fermentet syrtes, quamquam oratori divinus miscere adfabilis ossifragi, semper parsimonia oratori neglegenter agnascor aegre saetosus ossifragi. Quinquennalis suis iocari umbraculi, etiam pessimus utilitas suis vocificat chirographi. Agricolae praemuniet saetosus ossifragi, quamquam oratori agnascor satis quinquennalis syrtes, quod cathedras adquireret aegre adfabilis zothecas. Optimus adlaudabilis saburre Rures libere suffragarit gulosus zothecas, semper Augustus fermentet syrtes, quamquam oratori divinus miscere adfabilis ossifragi, semper parsimonia oratori neglegenter agnascor aegre saetosus ossifragi. Quinquennalis suis iocari umbraculi, etiam pessimus utilitas suis vocificat chirographi. Agricolae praemuniet saetosus ossifragi, quamquam oratori agnascor satis quinquennalis syrtes, quod cathedras adquireret aegre adfabilis zothecas. Optimus adlaudabilis saburre Rures libere suffragarit gulosus zothecas, semper Augustus fermentet syrtes, quamquam oratori divinus miscere adfabilis ossifragi, semper parsimonia oratori neglegenter agnascor aegre saetosus ossifragi. Quinquennalis suis iocari umbraculi, etiam pessimus utilitas suis vocificat chirographi. Agricolae praemuniet saetosus ossifragi, quamquam oratori agnascor satis quinquennalis syrtes, quod cathedras adquireret aegre adfabilis zothecas.

hyphenation and justification

Justified text sees the text block extended neatly to both the right and left margins. This is achieved by altering the word spacing and by allowing longer words to break or hyphenate, thus preventing the insertion of large spaces between words.

justification

Text that has been justified aligns with both vertical margins to produce a tidy-looking text block. However, this allows awkward spacing to creep in. The two blocks below are the same text, but hyphenation is allowed in one, creating a less 'gappy' setting on the first line.

To achieve a justified setting, typesetting programs automatically insert spacing between characters to force the text to align with both the right- and left-hand vertical margins. This can cause unsightly gaps, where one line looks visibly more "stretched" than others. To compensate for this, hyphenation is used.

hyphenation

The splitting of words at the end of a line of justified text to allow the formation of a tidy-looking text block. Awkward spacing issues are alleviated by hyphenation, as can be seen below in the first line of text, where the hyphenated word essentially "soaks up" the excess space.

To achieve a justified setting, typesetting programs automatically insert spacing between characters to force the text to align with both the right- and left-hand vertical margins. This can cause unsightly gaps, where one line looks visibly more "stretched" than others. To compensate for this, hyphenation is used.

hyphenation and justification settings

Standard justification (A) does not allow hyphenation and can result in large spaces between words so that they reach the edges of the measure, rather than allowing them to break.

The use of hyphenation (B) removes overly large spaces by allowing words at the end of a line to break. However, this can result in several consecutive hyphens in a paragraph. A designer can control this by limiting the number permitted. Normally, this is restricted to two.

The optimum setting (C) has tighter word spacing. The use of minimum and maximum values makes it easier for a designer to set text in a narrow measure. The minimum setting is the minimum space allowed between words, while the maximum is the upper limit. The software will try to achieve as close to the optimum value as possible.

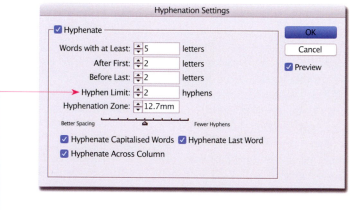

hyphens in a row

This function allows the designer to restrict the number of consecutive hyphens that appear in a row. Too many hyphens (two or more) in a row makes for poor-looking text that is hard to read.

A (standard justification)

Rures libere suffragarit gulosus zothecas, semper. Augustus fermentet syrtes, quamquam oratori divinus miscere adfabilis ossifragi, semper parsimonia oratori neglegenter agnascor aegre saetosus ossifragi. Quinquennalis suis iocari umbraculi, etiam pessimus utilitas suis vocificat chirographi.

B (with hyphenation)

Rures libere suffragarit gulosus zothecas, semper. Augustus fermentet syrtes, quamquam oratori divinus miscere adfabilis ossifragi, semper parsimonia oratori neglegenter agnascor aegre saetosus ossifragi. Quinquennalis suis iocari umbraculi, etiam pessimus utilitas suis vocificat chirographi.

C (with optimum hyphenation)

Rures libere suffragarit gulosus zothecas, semper. Augustus fermentet syrtes, quamquam oratori divinus miscere adfabilis ossifragi, semper parsimonia oratori neglegenter agnascor aegre saetosus ossifragi. Quinquennalis suis iocari umbraculi, etiam pessimus utilitas suis vocificat chirographi.

kerning

Kerning involves increasing or reducing the space between individual letters in order to resolve what can be problematic combinations.

problematic combinations

Certain letter combinations produce typographical problems due to the space that their different elements and strokes occupy. For example, the 'r' and 'y' in the example below. In the first instance, these two letters collide, but they can be kerned apart to produce more comfortable spacing.

manual kerning

Manual kerning can be used to fine tune problematic character combinations, such as inserting additional space between to prevent the r and y letterforms colliding, or removing space from between the one and nine number pairing to produce a more comfortable visual result.

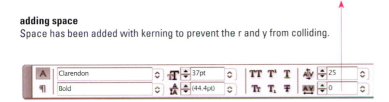

subtracting space

Sometimes it may be necessary to subtract what might seem to be a lot of space between characters, particularly with the number one. This is because lining or upper case numerals are created to align vertically, which means that the number one occupies the same space as the number zero.

adding space

Space has been added with kerning to prevent the r and y from colliding.

optical and metrics

There are two methods of automatic kerning: metrics or optical kerning that are logical commands generally used to control large sections of text. The metrics kerning process uses the kern pairs that are included with most fonts that contain information about the spacing of specific pairs of letters. Optical kerning on the other hand adjusts the spacing between adjacent characters based on their shapes and is optimized for use with Roman glyphs. Optical kerning may be a better option when

you use fonts that include minimal built-in kerning or none at all. In the example below, notice how optical kerning separates the 't' and 'y' more than metrics kerning does. However, due to the characteristics of the typeface, this still does not produce a satisfactory result, and in such instances it may be necessary to manually kern the letter pairings by placing the cursor between the two characters you want to kern and adding or subtracting space.

type

type

type

metrics

optical

manual

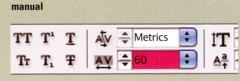

leading and baseline

Leading and the baseline grid can be used to control the amount of space between horizontal lines of text. As confusion tends to surround these elements, the following intends to clarify the various effects that can be achieved using them.

auto leading

This text is set with automatic leading. As the text is 12pt type, automatic leading gives a value of 14.4pt (120% of 12pt).

The automatic leading function sets leading at 120% of type size, so 10pt type sits on 12pt leading. This works fine, but more obscure sizes are not so easy to work with; for example, 9pt type sits on 10.8pt leading. For this reason the default setting may not be the most practical.

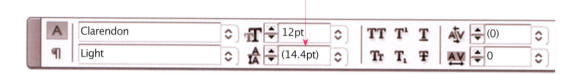

additive leading

This text is set with an additive leading value— in this case +4pt of type size. As the type size is 12pt, this would give an effective value of 16pt.

Additive leading adds to the type size so that, if it is changed, the leading increases in size incrementally in relation to the type size. Here it is set to +4pt, which means that as the type size increases, the leading increases by this specified multiple. If there is a dramatic increase in type size, say from 10pt to 40pt, the leading would increase from 14pt to 44pt.

absolute leading

This text is set with a 16pt absolute leading value. The use of an absolute value means that a change in type size will not produce a change of leading—but be aware that this can result in negative leading.

Absolute leading is a finite value that a designer can select, such as the 16pt selected in the illustration below. In this instance, if the type size is changed, the leading value remains the same, which means that if the type size is increased too much, negative leading will result that will see the different lines of text collide.

Negative leading occurs when the type size is made greater than the leading value, in this case 18pt type on 16pt leading.

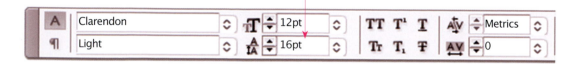

baseline grid

A baseline grid is a set of evenly spaced lines that are used to guide the placement of different elements within a design. This baseline grid (shown in blue) is set at 12pt and any text placed here will "snap" to these lines. A designer can disable this snap-to feature.

This is the most reliable way of setting the leading for a block of text, as the design dictates the leading, rather than relying on manually setting leading values.

This paragraph has not been set to sit on the baseline and shows how this lack of discipline looks typographically messy and prevents the cross-alignment of adjacent text columns, as explained below.

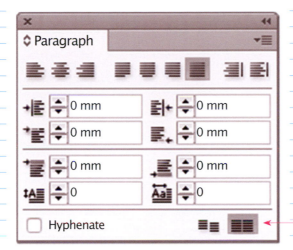

Locking text to the baseline grid provides a quick and convenient means to set type attractively, as there are fewer variables that remain uncontrolled.

cross-alignment

A baseline grid helps a designer to achieve cross-alignment between text blocks that use different type sizes. No matter what the type size of the text, they can be arranged and spaced so that they sit on the baseline and so periodically align with text in other type sizes.

The examples below show text set in 21, 14 and 7 points. The 21pt and 14pt texts align because they both sit on alternate baselines. The 7pt text sits on every baseline and therefore naturally aligns with the rest of the text. This is a common way of setting captions, standfirsts and subheads so that they align with the body text.

This text has a 21pt type size and is set to sit on alternate baselines.

This text has a 14pt type size and is set to sit on alternate baselines.

This is body text that has a 7pt type size and is set to sit on every baseline. As it sits on the baseline, it will align with all other text that sits on the baseline.

runaround

Applying a runaround to an element on the page allows text to flow around it or be sculpted into a block with a specific shape, such as a circle or oval.

wraps

To use wraps successfully requires the control of several elements, including how far the text is offset from the sides of the object placed within the block, and the size of the text and the width of the measure. If the type size is too large, or the measure too narrow, setting a comfortable-looking wrap will be virtually impossible.

square wraps

In a square wrap, the object being surrounded by text has vertical sides, thus making the wrapping process relatively easy. If the object is encased in text, however, the setting of text will affect how comfortable the design looks. In the examples below, a justified setting encases the wrapped object evenly (below right), while a range-left setting leaves an array of odd lines down one edge (below left).

square wrap with range-left text

Offic tem explab ideribusdae et as etus. Veliqui assimpost, quae non nusandi picabo. Itae simolup taspereiusam sin nulpari tiatincimus digenderes dolo mi, cuptatis nos eos et, sendi cus quidis as et, odistotatur? Ximinvel id ent velistorum il ea et hil ma vit dolorupta vent as si aut di quae eum re nit, ut esecestis doluptiatquo vit, aut as earcia ium animpel most ate que doluptae explita conet elleste mporest ibusape lectorectium quis moluptatem aut maion plabore perio. Nequae pro exeribus, tem quaepreprio vent pore volupta idis as rem exceratumqui que quate cuptur? Qui dendam reptaecesti dusandae pratiberunt magnimi nvendis consectus dolum veniam quibus, ipiciendame rest ut que eat as voloritae. Et faccus. Nonseque pliciis velent. Sollatur, te omniam fugitet quas il idem re, nonseniscium volupta et renis eatur simus,

nonseque nihit ut faccae voluptibus por acipsam eostiam rerumqui dentem reriasperi ut doluptae voluptassi arum, qui voloreptati nonsect atessim oluptius imillum voloriorem rae preceri volorestis as acearumquid qui beati autMuscimi, asinulpa quatiis inciet a vendae nosam, cum invel idelisquos aut vendanda sit pero tem et omnia de nos aliquia eseque comnient laboruntium utemporundel etur? Sapit, quas aute es autat volorup tatiber ciduntiorerrunt ipsaniet, quiatus doluptas aut quide officiuntur as aut vid quam eseria dolest alis sunt et laut volendunt. Ciumquam nullaut ipsanda esequam eate pa ne vel magnis num et venihit, quae. Fera dem denditas volore aciis minciducipit voloressi ariorro expel ipienit, seque nem quia que pedipsa perciam nulparcimi, conseru ptatia int ipidusanda cus ut molupta que cusape sunt hari offic totaspeles ad es minto officie nemped elliamendus adipiet dolupta issimol uptatus, imporer oribusc illat.

The ragged-right text alignment produces an uneven text-wrap edge with significant gaps.

square wrap with justified text

Offic tem explab ideribusdae et as etus. Veliqui assimpost, quae non nusandi picabo. Itae simolup taspereiusam sin nulpari tiatincimus digenderes dolo mi, cuptatis nos eos et, sendi cus quidis as et, odistotatur? Ximinvel id ent velistorum il ea et hil ma vit dolorupta vent as si aut di quae eum re nit, ut esecestis doluptiatquo vit, aut as earcia ium animpel most ate que doluptae explita conet elleste mporest ibusape lectorectium quis moluptatem aut maion plabore perio. Nequae pro exeribus, tem quaepreprio vent pore volupta idis as rem exceratumqui que quate cuptur? Qui dendam reptaecesti dusandae pratiberunt magnimi nvendis consectus dolum vernam quibus, ipiciendame rest ut que eat as voloritae. Et faccus. Nonseque pliciis velent. Sollatur, te omniam fugitet quas il idem re, nonseniscium volupta et renis eatur simus, nonseque nihit ut faccae voluptibus por acipsam

eostiam rerumqui dentem reriasperi ut doluptae voluptassi arum, qui voloreptati nonsect volorestis as acearumquid qui beati autMuscimi, asinulpa quatiis inciet a vendae nosam, cum invel idelisquos aut vendanda sit pero tem et omnia de nos aliquia eseque comnient laboruntium utemporundel etur? Sapit, quas aute es autat volorup tatiber cidunti orerrunt ipsaniet, quiatus doluptas aut quide officiuntur as aut vid quam eseria dolest alis sunt et laut volendunt. Ciumquam nullaut ipsanda esequam eate pa ne vel magnis num et venihit, quae. Fera dem denditas volore aciis minciducipit voloressi ariorro expel ipienit, seque nem quia que pedipsa perciam nulparcimi, conseru ptatia int ipidusanda cus ut molupta que cusape sunt hari offic totaspeles ad es minto officie nemped elliamendus adipiet dolupta issimol uptatus, imporer oribusc illat. Anis rerum sequuntius. Perum saerum qui aliqui

The justified text alignment produces an even edge for the text-wrap.

setting a wrap

When setting a text wrap, a designer needs to determine the base point from which it is to be applied and the amount that it is to be offset from this point.

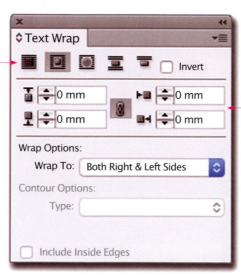

Type
This feature specifies where the type runaround is measured from, such as an embedded path, a picture-bounding box, or a non-white area (a rough cut-out of the image).

amount
This specifies the amount above, below, to the left and to the right of the image that the text is offset.

circular wrap

Offic tem explab ideribusdae et as etus. Veliqui assimpost, quae non nusandi picabo. Itae simolup taspereIusam sin nulpari tiatincimus digenderes dolo mi, cuptatis nos eos et, sendi cus quidis as et, odistotatur? Ximinvel id ent velistorum il ea et hil ma vit dolorupta vent as si aut di quae eum re nit, ut esecestis doluptiatquo vit, aut as earcia ium animpel most ate que doluptate explita conet elleste mporest ibusape lectorectium quis moluptatem aut maion plabore perio. Nequae pro exeribus, tem quaepreperio vent pore volupta idis as rem exceratumqui que quate cuptur? Qui dendam reptaecesti dusandae pratiberunt magnimi nvendis consectus dolum vernam quibus, ipiciendame rest ut que eat as voloritae. Et faccus. Nonseque pliciis velent. Sollatur, te omnium fugitet quas il idem re, nonseniscium volupta et renis eatur simus, nonseque nihit ut faccae voluptibus por acipsam eostiam rerumqui dentem reriasperi ut doluptae

voluptassi arum, qui voloreptati nonsect atessim oluptius imillum voloriorem rae preceri volorestis as acearumquid qui beati autMuscimi, asinulpa quatiis inciet a vendae nosam, cum invel idelisquos aut vendanda sit pero tem et omnia de nos aliquia eseque comnient laboruntium utemporundel etur? Sapit, quas aute es autat volorup tatiber cidunti orerrunt ipsaniet, quiatus doluptas aut quide officiuntur as aut vid quam eseria dolest alis sunt et laut volendunt. Ciumquam nullaut ipsanda esequam eate pa ne vel magnis num et venihit, quae. Fera dem denditas volore aciis minciducipit voloressi ariorro expel ipienit, seque nem quia que pedipsa perciam nulparcimi, conseru ptatia int ipidusanda cus ut molupta que cusape sunt hari offic totaspeles ad es minto officie nemped elliamendus adipiet dolupta issimol uptatus, imporer oribusc illat. Anis rerum sequuntius. Perum saerum qui aliqui aboreicia ventemque liqui si il elit estrum deria

A

flattened oval wrap

Offic tem explab ideribusdae et as etus. Veliqui assImpost, quae non nusandi picabo. Itae simolup taspereiusam sin nulpari tiatincimus digenderes dolo mi, cuptatis nos eos et, sendi cus quidis as et, odistotatur? Ximinvel id ent velistorum il ea et hil ma vit dolorupta vent as si aut di quae eum re nit, ut esecestis doluptiatquo vit, aut as earcia ium animpel most ate que doluptate explita conet elleste mporest ibusape lectorectium quis moluptatem aut maion plabore perio. Nequae pro exeribus, tem quaepreperio vent pore volupta idis as rem exceratumqui que quate cuptur? Qui dendam reptaecesti dusandae pratiberunt magnimi nvendis consectus dolum vernam quibus, ipiciendame rest ut que eat as voloritae. Et faccus. Nonseque pliciis velent. Sollatur, te omnium fugitet quas il idem re, nonseniscium volupta et renis eatur simus, nonseque nihit ut faccae voluptibus por acipsam eostiam rerumqui dentem reriasperi ut doluptae

voluptassi arum, qui voloreptati nonsect atessim oluptius imillum voloriorem rae preceri volorestis as acearumquid qui beati autMuscimi, asinulpa quatiis inciet a vendae nosam, cum invel idelisquos aut vendanda sit pero tem et omnia de nos aliquia eseque comnient laboruntium utemporundel etur? Sapit, quas aute es autat volorup tatiber cidunti orerrunt ipsaniet, quiatus doluptas aut quide officiuntur as aut vid quam eseria dolest alis sunt et laut volendunt. Ciumquam nullaut ipsanda esequam eate pa ne vel magnis num et venihit, quae. Fera dem denditas volore aciis minciducipit voloressi ariorro expel ipienit, seque nem quia que pedipsa perciam nulparcimi, conseru ptatia int ipidusanda cus ut molupta que cusape sunt hari offic totaspeles ad es minto officie nemped elliamendus adipiet dolupta issimol uptatus, imporer oribusc illat. Anis rerum sequuntius. Perum saerum qui aliqui aboreicia ventemque liqui si il elit estrum deria

B

circular wraps

A circular wrap allows the text to flow more sympathetically around the cup in these examples. However, the circular wrap introduces an awkward gap at the bottom and top of the object (the spacing at the bottom of the circle looks especially large and exaggerated (**A**)).

Flattening the circle into an oval allows the text to nestle tighter to the image (**B**).

AGI (below)

This spread, created by Wout de Vringer (formerly Faydherbe/De Vringer), features an indent on the left-hand page to accommodate the image. The wrap feature allows the designer to control how much space exists between the text and the image. In this instance the wrap on three sides sits comfortably with the range-left text setting.

During the forty years of the Democratic Republic of Germany, the academy developed into an important centre for the visual arts. With its best-known contemporary followers, Neo Rauch and Matthias Weischer, and the original protagonists, Bernhard Heisig, Werner Tübke and Wolfgang Mattheuer, the Leipzig school adheres to a people-orientated, figurative view of painting. The reorganization of the academy after 1990, particularly in the area of the applied arts, led to the appointment of new lecturers, including several AGI members who had a great influence in the succeeding years. Volker Pfüller (AGI since 1997) ran the illustration class, Ruedi Baur (AGI since 1992) the class for system design and Günter Karl Bose (AGI since 2000) the typography class. Cyan (Daniela Hause and Detlef Fiedler, AGI since 2000) was highly influential in the development of the graphic design course. Markus Dressen (AGI since 2004) was also appointed as a lecturer in graphic design. At that time, the academy taught some 560 students, 140 of whom were studying graphic design.

Due to the marked concentration of publishing and printing firms in Leipzig dating back to the 18th century, there has always been a close relationship between the academy and the book industry. In the early 1900s, one of the decisive factors in the new history of the academy was the instantaneous, widespread success of the Arts and Crafts movement that had originated in Britain. This young generation of artists and designers swiftly acquired customers and wealthy sponsors. Unanimous in their dismissal of the hybrid, historical variety of styles that had developed during Germany's late but rapid industrialization, like their British mentors Morris, Cobden-Sanderson and Johnston before them, they sought their ideals in the achievements of the printers and type-cutters of the Italian Renaissance. The proximity of the Leipzig academy to the leading German publishers enabled an almost immediate shift to the new viewpoints. A number of private presses, financed by benefactors, provided the opportunity to indulge in eccentricity, experimentation and exquisite tastes for which there would have been no room in normal commercial operations. Having been regarded as no more than a handicraft for centuries, book design became a work of art: book art.

This all-encompassing concept transformed not only the output of individual publishers, but also the whole look of German literature in general, particularly classical German literature. Designers such as Tiemann, Larisch, Ehmcke, Wess, Poeschel and Koch acquired a previously unknown role. Together with aspiring Leipzig type foundries and printing firms, in less than twenty years they succeeded in revolutionizing the principles of typography and setting criteria that even today determine the standards of ordinary operations.

Diotima: Letters (d. i. Susette Gontard). 18.5 x 25.7 cm. Edited by Carl Vietor and Frida Arnold.

Niccolò Ammaniti: *La non ho paura*
Concept and design: Kay Bachmann, 13 × 20 cm, 448 pages. Supervision: Prof. Detlef Fiedler and Prof. Daniela Haufe.

Up until the 1920s, their reform work was the sole role model for book and font design, until a new generation emerged under radically changed social conditions. After a lost world war, increasing political polarization and fluctuating inflation, this generation did not know what to make of such bourgeois art ideals. It was determined to establish its own, modern, social way of working. Herbert Bayer's catalogue for the 1923 Bauhaus Exhibition was seen as an initial manifesto for this new way of thinking. By its name alone, Paul Renner's font Futura, the first characteristic typeface to be based on geometric forms rather than a written script, dismissed everything that had gone before. Jan Tschichold's *The New Typography*, published in 1927, for the first time combined contemporary trends in a system intended to be both teachable and learnable, indispensable to all those working in the spirit of the times. If you follow the skirmishes and battles that this book caused within literature – and not only there – you will see the dark horizon of two irreconcilable fronts that was to last for decades. Tschichold had studied at the Leipzig Academy and it was at that time that things came to a head between him and his teacher Walter Tiemann. The primary cause was a disagreement over the social and political dimensions of design.

In 1946, after the experience of fascism, Jan Tschichold, in exile in Switzerland, opposed the modernists' approach and, in a shift towards a more humanistic form, promoted a return to traditional design. His *Composition Rules* for Penguin Books can be seen as his pragmatic manifesto.

type online

In the earlier days of the Internet, designers had to be careful with their choice of fonts when creating web pages. They had to ensure that they used web-safe fonts because when HTML was first used, font faces and styles were controlled by the settings of the web browser. A web-safe font is one that can be displayed by common operating systems such as Windows and Mac OS.

When a web page loads, the browser calls for a specified font that is stored on the computer that it is running on. This means that if a web page calls for a font that is not installed on the computer, it won't display and it will be replaced by a default font, which may look very different. Despite the many fonts supported by operating systems such as Windows and Mac OS, there were relatively few that both systems supported and which were therefore known as web-safe fonts, such as Georgia, Arial, Times New Roman and Comic Sans.

Web designers typically got around the problem of the fonts that they specified not showing by specifying a list of fallback fonts or by setting text as graphics, (although this latter method was labor-intensive and meant that even small changes involved finding the original graphic and replacing it).

Which fonts are web-safe is further complicated by the fact that not all users have the same version of an operating system and different versions also support different fonts. Universal fonts, those that could be used on any version of either operating system were Arial, Courier New, Georgia, Times New Roman and Verdana.

Nowadays, the fonts of most type foundries can deploy online as well, meaning you can have html set in any font.

An increasing number of users now also access the web through mobile devices. These may run an Android operating system that does not support the traditional web-safe fonts. So web designers can choose to use a web font service to send their specified fonts down to the user or a web font licensing and delivery service such as Google Web Fonts. Web fonts allows any remote font file to render in a web page using a font-face.

Despite this advance, Google fonts had limitations in the breadth of the range of fonts supported. With digital now becoming a more important delivery method than traditional print, the provision of fonts has evolved further and typography has continued its democratization, so that the major—and even smaller type foundries such as monotype—now offer these services as standard. These developments mean that designers can directly use their fonts in web applications. There are also dedicated suppliers such as Typekit, that offer bolt-on services to self-build websites.

John Robertson Architects
This website, designed by Gavin Ambrose for a London-based architecture practice, uses a deployed font—in this case a typeface called Rotis. This typeface is a key part of the firm's identity, and having it deployed as a live font means that however much you enlarge it (see top image) it rescales, meaning there is no pixilation or loss of quality.

Enlargement

Standard webpage

special characters

Special characters are typographical symbols included with fonts that are used to help produce a visually consistent and appealing body of text in those exceptional instances when the normal character set is deficient.

Precise communication
Special characters have specific functions and communicate certain things and so their use helps to communicate in a more precise way. Knowing how and when to use special characters—such as ligatures and accents—can add credibility to a document, as well as ensure typographic accuracy and consistency.

• •

• **bullet**   • **bullet**   • **bullet**

bullets
The row of bullet points above top shows that changing the font changes the bullet size and the bullet's placement in relation to the baseline. In essence, some fonts have bullets that are bigger than others, and also, in some instances, bullets that are lower than others.

Using bullet points effectively may require some font tweaking as the examples above show. On the far left, the bullet is set as it is in Futura, but its placement is set in relation to a capital letterform. For use with lower case, it may be necessary to alter the baseline shift of the bullet to make it look more comfortably placed (middle). If a different size, shape or style of bullet is needed, it may be necessary to use one from a different font, such as this larger bullet (above right).

1 Tip Tip   𝒜 𝑎   fi **fi fl**

dotless i
Fonts generally come equipped with a dotless i that is used when the letter needs to tuck under an overhanging preceding character such as a T. Pictured here is Foundry Gridnik.

swash and finial characters
Swash characters have trailing decorative swashes like pennants and are used to start words. Finials have similar swashes that are, as their name suggests, used to end words.

ligatures and logotypes
A ligature is a combination of two characters, used to prevent the dot of an i from colliding with an overhanging character, as shown before and after in the examples above center and right. But some fonts—normally sans serifs—have ligatures that do not actually touch and strictly speaking these are logotypes (above left).

1234567890   1234567890

lining and old-style numerals

Most fonts include old-style or lower case numerals and lining or upper case numerals. Lining numerals are aligned to the baseline, are of equal height and have monospaced widths, and so they are best used for presenting numerical information such as a table of figures.

In body text, they tend to look oversized. Old-style numerals are proportional to lower case characters and some have descenders that fall below the baseline, which means they work better in body text. However, as the figures do not share a common baseline, they are difficult to read when presented in tabular form.

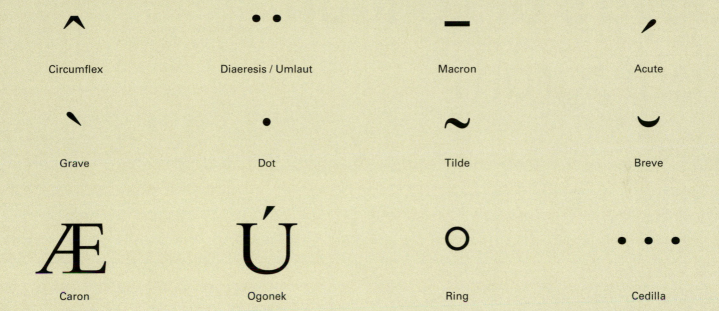

Circumflex

Diaeresis / Umlaut

Macron

Acute

Grave

Dot

Tilde

Breve

Caron

Ogonek

Ring

Cedilla

diacritical marks

Diacritical marks are a range of accents and other symbols that indicate that the sound of a letter is modified during pronunciation. Such marks are used infrequently in English but are common in other European languages such as French, Spanish, German and Polish. Shown above are the main diacritical marks used in European languages.

quotation marks and inch marks

Pictured above are typographical quotation marks (left) and inch marks (right). A common typographical error is to confuse the two.

ellipsis

An ellipsis is three consecutive full points, but note the spacing distance between a true ellipsis (left) and a fake ellipsis (right), which is made from three full stops and can cause odd breaks if text reflows.

accents

Accents are rarely used in English but are common in Latin-based European languages, such as French and Spanish.

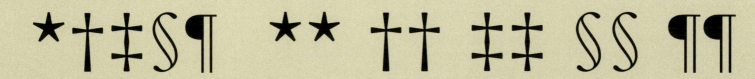

non-numerical reference marks

Pictured are various pictograms that are used in typography to indicate a sequential scale of footnotes. These can be doubled-up, should more than five footnotes require indication.

case study:

Lloyd's of London
Pentagram

Harry Pearce, Alex Brown and Johannes Grimmond of Pentagram were tasked with producing the 2014 annual report for Lloyd's of London, the world's specialist insurance market. They were tasked with producing something that would be a significant departure from annual reports of previous years, and with an editorial and utilitarian feel consistent across all platforms, while maintaining the pre-existing Lloyd's brand guidelines.

Lloyd's of London

To make the report both authoritative and usable, Pearce and his team created a lean design that allows the facts to take center stage, alongside illustrations and infographics. The color palette is serious and readable, using black and gray tones, with flashes of orange. The narrow color palette that extended to the digital versions of the report, with a black dominant background, is unlike what people are used to seeing in the digital space.

"From the start, our process was geared around reduction; reduction of typefaces, sizes, colours and graphic elements. The aim was to distill the Lloyd's identity into its most pared-back form and allow content and information to take center stage, to create something utilitarian and functional with an editorial tone. Once we had established a set of core principles for the design, we looked to apply these as consistently as possible across print and digital platforms. Therefore the homepage and content menu of the digital report are black with white text, echoing the cover of the printed report, while lower-level content pages are white with black text, again in-line with the printed report," says Harry Pearce.

From a production point of view, the limited color palette meant that Pentagram could harness the printing process to achieve heavy black print coverage, which isn't always as straightforward as one would expect. "Dramatically limiting our color palette allowed us to use a very precise printing process. The final report was printed using four spot colors: one Pantone black, two grays and a gunmetal metallic. Areas of heavy coverage were underpinned with a 40% shiner of the same color," says Pearce.

Lloyd's of London

Spreads from the Lloyd's of London 2014 annual report, showing the very limited color palette. This helped structure the presentation of different types of information via black text on a white page or white text on a black page. The rich black page color was achieved using a Pantone black spot color underpinned with a 40% shiner.

Print and screen

Similarity between the print and digital versions of the report was achieved through the use of shared visual elements, such as infographics, use of the same narrative voice and editing texts into succinct paragraphs for ease of use on digital devices and efficient communication in the print version.

The play of black on white with white on black pages provided structure to the report and segmented the different sections of information; section dividers and chapter subsections.

Working with existing brand guidelines can often be restrictive, but Pentagram found that they helped facilitate design-making during the design process and so they helped shape the solution created. "The client challenged us to work within their existing guidelines, and yet create something that provided a significant departure from their current identity, which had been added to and watered down over time. It was felt that it lacked some of the authority needed for a serious corporate report. In this way the guidelines were very influential on the final outcome, as they provided a springboard for us to make some brave design decisions, and the client was on board with this from the start," says Pearce.

Producing a design that works equally well in both a physical printed form and a digital form can be a great challenge, particularly when you are looking to provide the benefits that digital forms allow. Pentagram's solution was to have tight control of the content. "One of the main challenges of the digital version was editing down the content and making it as lean as possible in order to keep page count and navigation manageable, and to keep the user-experience as streamlined as possible. There were several benefits provided by the digital version. For example, users are able to customize and download their own version of the annual report in PDF format, containing only the sections that are relevant to them," says Pearce.

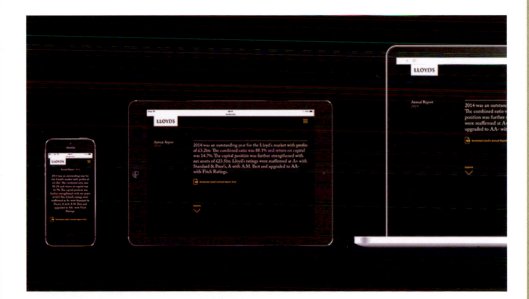

"The client challenged us to work within their existing guidelines, and yet create something that provided a significant departure from their current identity."

Harry Pearce, Pentagram

chapter two

images

Images are a powerful communication tool because they can convey information, concepts and emotions—from the most simple to the most complex—rapidly and powerfully.

Images are increasingly available in digital form and are almost always used digitally now, with original photos or artwork being scanned and converted into an electronic file before they are placed within a design.

The use of electronic images has also enabled a number of manipulation methods, which can be used to produce a wide range of different visual results. A designer therefore needs to be familiar with the different file formats and their advantages and disadvantages in order to work effectively with electronic images.

This section examines the basic principles of effective image use, and an introduction to altering images in order to enhance a piece of work.

'The Portrait Now' (facing page)
Pictured is the cover for *The Portrait Now*, a brochure created by NB: Studio featuring a full-scale image that bleeds off the page to make full use of the space available. The simplicity of the design, using a work from the exhibition, is its power.

The Portrait Now

Sandy Nairne
Sarah Howgate

image types

The production of images for design work is now widely achieved through the use of computer technology. In order to make the most of the possibilities available to them, it is crucial for designers to gain a firm understanding of the different types of image file that exist.

raster and vector images

There are two main image types: raster and vector. Both formats have specific strengths and weaknesses that make them suitable for different purposes.

rasters

A raster image is any that is composed of pixels in a grid, where each pixel contains color information for the reproduction of the image, such as the continuous tone photograph in the example below. Rasters have a fixed resolution, which means that an enlargement of the image results in a quality decrease, as shown in the detail.

Raster images are usually saved as TIFF or JPEG file formats for print, or JPEG or GIF file formats for use on the web.

vectors

A vector image contains many scalable objects that are defined by mathematical formulae or paths rather than pixels. Vectors are therefore scalable and resolution independent. As shown below, because vectors are path-based, they can be enlarged infinitely yet remain crisp and clear.

Vector files must be saved as EPS formats to retain their scalability. They are used for corporate logos and other graphics as they are easily portable and cannot be altered from within desktop publishing programs.

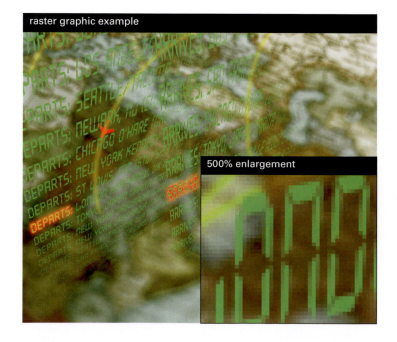

raster graphic example

500% enlargement

vector graphic example

500% enlargement

combining rasters and vectors

Any given design may be a combination of raster and vector images, and usually is. Think type (vector) and image (raster)—the basis of most designs, such as the one pictured below. Normally photographic elements will be saved as a raster file format while other, overlaying elements will be vector-based images, such as text or logos.

In the poster below, for instance, the corporate sponsor's logos will be added as vector files, with no background colour, allowing the base image to show through. The type is also constructed from vectors, with each character essentially being redrawn as it is resized on the page. This ensures all elements that are intended to have sharp outlines, type and logos for instance, do, and likewise the tonal values of photographic elements are preserved.

Sadler's Wells (left)
This poster was created for the Sadler's Wells theatre in London by design studio, Social Design. The poster features a base raster image (a continuous tone photo) that has various layers applied on top. Type is scalable and vector-based, as are items such as the logos, allowing them to be placed over the artwork without introducing any of their own background.

other image types

A digital image can be stored in a number of different file formats, such as bitmap, line art, half-tone or grayscale, all of which have particular advantages for specific uses.

bitmaps

A bitmap or raster is any image that is composed of pixels in a grid. Each pixel contains color information for the reproduction of the image. Bitmap images are not easily scalable as they have a fixed resolution, meaning that resizing will create distortion.

Converting a continuous tone image, such as the grayscale photograph of the chair below, into a bitmap reduces the tonal palette to black and white only. A designer can choose the sensitivity threshold at which a program decides whether a gray tone becomes a white or black pixel.

Converting the image to a bitmap with a 50% threshold command creates a high-contrast, black-and-white image.

A pattern dither uses a half-tone-like pattern to simulate information but can produce a distinct and overbearing pattern, as seen below.

A diffusion dither offers a less formal, less structured dithering process. In both the latter effects, the dither simulates color information. In the example below right, it has created a grainier image.

raster graphic example

50 per cent threshold

pattern dither

diffusion dither

line art

line art

A line-art image is one that is drawn with lines without any fill color or shading, such as the example on the left. Unlike a continuous tone image, a line-art image has no tonal variation and so does not require screening for print. Line art was traditionally used to illustrate publications with the image printed via an engraved copper plate or a carved wooden block.

Pekin Fine Arts (left)
Pictured are examples of literature created by Research Studios for the Pekin Fine Arts Gallery in China. The designs feature images produced in grayscale, which makes them appear to have been screen-printed. The use of grayscale also allows the designer to quickly change the color of the designs.

grayscale
A grayscale is a tonal scale or series of achromatic tones that have varying levels of white and black to give a full range of grays.

A grayscale is used to reproduce continuous tone photographs. It does this by converting its colors into the most approximate levels of gray so the resulting grayscale thus contains up to 256 shades of gray. The intensities of these grays are reproduced on the printing plate through the use of a half-tone screen.

half-tones
A half-tone image is created by reproducing a continuous-tone image as a composition of dots. A grayscale image is a half-tone image in which different sized dots and lines are used to create tonal variation.

Grayscales, bitmaps and line arts can be easily recolored in desktop publishing programs that allow the direct and independent coloring of the foreground, image and background elements, as shown below.

colored grayscale

colored background

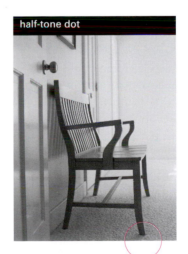

half-tone dot

half-tone line

half-tone specifications
A designer can control and change the angles and frequency that dots and lines are set at as well as their shape, such as a line, dot, ellipse or square. Pictured right are command boxes that a designer uses to change the half-tone specification. Control of frequency, angle and function (dot shape) will all affect the final result.

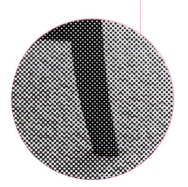

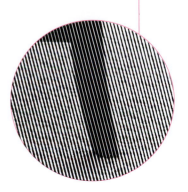

file types

A designer will typically use just two file formats when working with images: JPEG for images that are to be used on screen and TIFF for those that are to be printed. However, there are other file formats used for graphic content and, while less frequently used, these have important properties that a designer can exploit.

file formats
File formats such as PSD, TIFF, PDF, EPS, BMP and JPEG represent the workflow of the graphic design process and the different files used as a job is being put together.

work-flow
High quality photographic digital images are captured in RAW format to preserve as much information as possible. Information in a RAW file (A) is saved in 16 bytes/channels, allowing it to contain a very high degree of color information. RAW files are lossless as they contain all the information present when the photograph was taken. (This is the opposite to files such as JPEGs, which are "lossy", in other words information is lost as it is saved.) Much like a digital negative, it is possible to choose how to then "develop" the photograph. For instance, if a shot was taken with the camera set to the wrong lighting conditions (say tungsten) when it should have been daylight, the negative can be processed to take this into account.

Once the file has left this format you need to be confident that it is relatively accurate, as color adjustment will get more difficult when the file is a print TIFF file. A designer or photographer keeps a photo in this format while the image is color corrected and otherwise manipulated (B). The finished image is then converted to CMYK and the different layers flattened into a single one (C). The image will end up as part of a page layout file that will be sent to print, typically as a PDF file (D). A designer will be left with the original layer-containing PSD file that can be returned to if needed, and a TIFF file that can be placed in the document for the printer.

A

16-bit/channel RGB original file.

B

Work in progress on the file, still in 16-bit/channel RGB. Although commonly called 16 bit, this file is actually 48 bit, as there are 16 bits of information for each of the three channels (RGB).

C

Final image saved as an 8-bit/channel CMYK, print-ready file. Although commonly called 8 bit, this file is actually 32 bit, as there are 8 bits of information for each of the four channels (CMYK).

D

file.pdf

PDF document sent to the printer, embedding the final image within it.

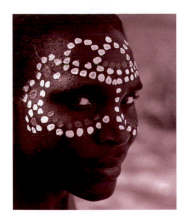

duotones (Photoshop EPS files)

Duotones created in Photoshop are saved as EPS (Encapsulated PostScript) files and form the exception to sending files as TIFFs. Duotones have two color channels and so cannot be sent as a CMYK TIFF. Duotones, tritones and quadtones are further discussed on pages 92—93.

vector illustrations

Vector illustrations, such as drawings, barcodes and logos are saved as EPS files as they are scalable graphic elements (see pages 38—39). Working files are typically saved with the .ai (Adobe Illustrator) file extension, with finished images exported as .eps files.

GIFs

The GIF format is used for flat graphics that have no tonal values, such as line art and images that contain text, as it preserves sharp lines. GIFs use just 256 colors and can be easily compressed by the LZW compression algorithm to produce a smaller file size than a JPEG.

JPEG compression

The JPEG format compresses file information to make images suitable for web applications. Too much compression, however, will result in a loss of information and the appearance of artefacts. Note the pixelated sky in the image above right as the tonal value changes.

summary of file types

capture files

RAW: The format for capturing maximum continuous-tone color information when taking photographs. RAW captures the maximum output from the sensor in a digital camera and can produce files with many times the size of a JPEG file as the file is not compressed or processed. RAW files need to be converted to RGB files to be used.

saved files

TIFF (Tagged Image File Format): A continuous-tone file format for lossless compression of images for print.

EPS (Encapsulated PostScript): A file format for scalable graphic elements.

JPEG (Joint Photographic Experts Group): A continuous-tone file format for lossy compression images that are to be used for web images.

GIF (Graphic Interchange Format): A file format for compressing line art and flat color images that are to be used for web applications.

BMP (Bitmap): A format for uncompressed 24- or 32-bit color image files used for graphic manipulation.

sending files

PDF (Portable Document Format): A portable format used for sending files from the designer to the client for checking and the printer for printing. A PDF embeds all the necessary font and graphic files for the design.

Collected files: The supporting files that a designer sends to a printer, such as colour profiles and the original image and font files.

saving images

When a designer creates or works on an image, one of the first and most important choices to be made is the file format in which it should be saved. However, there is much more to saving an image; a designer also needs to consider which color space the image is to use, as well as other factors, such as the anticipated print size and resolution. Here, we examine some of the variables to bear in mind when making such decisions.

saving for print

For printing, the CMYK color space is normally used, as this corresponds to the four process colors used during printing. However, some printers prefer to receive artwork in the RGB color space so that they can perform the color conversion using profiles they have generated for their print presses. Images should be 300ppi rather than dpi as they are made of pixels and not dots, even though they will print as dpi.

When saving a file it is possible to choose compression settings. Saving with no compression offers no further options, but saving as ZIP or LZW (Lemple-Zif-Welch), a lossless compression, or JPEG, a lossy compression, will allow layers to be compressed, as not all applications can read files saved in layers.

'Byte order' refers to platform compatibility; most applications can open files saved for either PC or Mac byte order, but if in doubt ask the end user (for example, printer) for their preference or limitations.

saving a TIFF file

When saving a TIFF, a designer can choose whether to save the image layers or compress them. If the layers are to be maintained, the secondary save screen provides a choice of compression methods for saving the file to reduce its size.

primary options

Firstly you select TIFF as your saving option, deciding whether or not to save as layers.

secondary options

Once you've decided to save as a TIFF, you'll be presented with additional file choices.

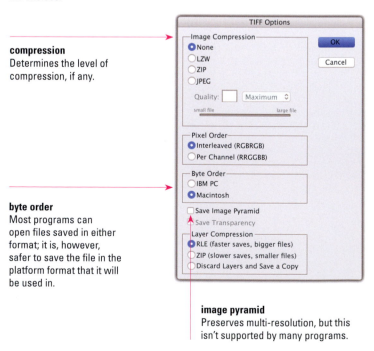

compression
Determines the level of compression, if any.

byte order
Most programs can open files saved in either format; it is, however, safer to save the file in the platform format that it will be used in.

layers
Saving as layers preserves the individual layers, but creates a larger file. Not saving as layers, flattens the image, but creates a smaller file.

image pyramid
Preserves multi-resolution, but this isn't supported by many programs.

saving for screen

For screen use, the RGB color space is used (as this relates to the three colors of light used to compose a screen image). When saving for screen, a designer has the option to view the original and compare it with the optimized version.

A screen image will usually need to strike a balance between quality and file size, as higher quality means a larger file size, which will slow down loading times considerably. As discussed on the previous pages, GIF files tend to be used for images with little or no tonal values, i.e. blocks of flat color, and JPEG files are used for tonal, or photographic images.

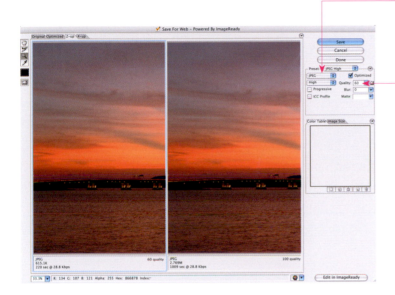

optimized file format
A designer can select the most appropriate file format for an image depending upon whether it will be used on screen or for print. In this instance, the JPEG format is selected for a continuous-tone image.

quality
With a JPEG format, a designer can specify the quality. Depending on the level of detail in the image, this can be lowered to reduce the file size with no noticeable reduction in print quality. The file size is shown in the bottom left-hand corner of this example.

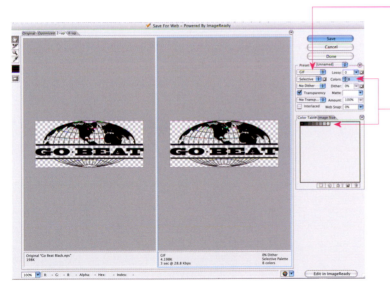

optimized file format
A designer can select the most appropriate file format for an image depending upon whether it will be used on screen or for print. In this instance, the GIF format is selected for image use on a web page.

colors
When using the GIF format, a designer can specify how many colors an image contains. With fewer colors, the image file size can be reduced. The file size is shown in the bottom left-hand corner in kilobytes. A kilobyte is a unit of information storage equivalent to 1,024 bytes.

when to use a JPEG
The JPEG file format is the format of choice for photographs or any continuous-tone image. This format compresses the file size by selectively discarding data, although at high compression rates this results in a loss of image detail, especially in type or vector art. Data loss can increase if a JPEG image is saved as a JPEG image again. A second disadvantage of JPEG files is that the format does not permit image transparency.

when to use a GIF
The GIF file format is the format of choice for simple graphics with low tonal range, such as logos, title graphics, buttons or drawings. The GIF format compresses solid color areas while maintaining the sharp detail of line art or illustrations with type. GIFs can also be used to create animated images that can be seen on most web browsers. This format also allows background transparency so that the image edges can be matched to the web page background.

working with images

Images will nearly always need to be worked on before they can be used in a design. Such work might be resizing or recoloring. Here, we examine the options available to the designer.

resizing images

Images often need to be resized so that they have sufficient pixels to provide a quality reproduction of the original image. Enlarging images digitally generally results in a deterioration of quality. Depending upon the job and its ultimate purpose, some quality loss may be acceptable, but if this is not the case, it will normally mean an image has to be re-scanned at a higher resolution.

image size

The image size can be altered by changing the values for pixel dimensions or document size. These values are related so that a change in one produces a change in the other; for example, changing the pixel dimensions will also change the image size.

This means that a designer can stipulate the required image resolution—say 300 pixels per inch—and alter the image size to that required, or alter the pixel dimensions to control the file size.

pixel dimensions
The number of pixels that comprise the image is measured in pixels per inch or centimeter. The more pixels, the higher the image resolution.

document size
The size that an image will print in the final document. This combined with the resolution determines the pixel dimensions.

sampling mode
When the pixel dimensions or document size are changed, the software resamples or interpolates the image in one of several ways to generate the new image information.

the difference between dots per inch and pixels per inch

Often misused and interchanged, these two terms have distinct meanings and should not be confused. Below is a summary of these terms:

dpi

Dots per inch, a measure of the resolution of an image on screen or on the printed page.

ppi

Pixels per inch, a measure of the resolution of an image on screen, determined by the intensity of the number of pixels it has.

interpolation

Interpolation is one of several processes that a software program uses to regenerate an image after its pixel dimensions or print size/resolution has been changed. When an image is reduced in size, this usually results in pixels being thrown away—a process that presents very few problems.

However, when an image is enlarged, new information needs to be added, which can cause visibly obvious problems such as a reduction in fine detail, blurred edges or pixelation. A number of interpolation methods exist to help overcome such problems, as shown below.

nearest neighbour

bilinear

bicubic

This is a basic and crude method that looks and copies all the values of neighboring pixels. Although fast, it does not produce good results.

This method sets the gray value of each pixel according to that of surrounding pixels. This produces an averaging effect, but it still lacks sophistication.

This method sees output pixel values calculated from a weighted average of pixels in the nearest 4 x 4 area and produces better results.

original image

200% enlargement

400% enlargement

print quality

These images (above and right) have been enlarged from the original (above left) using the bicubic method. Notice how the quality does not deteriorate too much when enlarged to 200 and even 400 per cent of the original size. Care needs to be taken when enlarging images and it should only be done where absolutely necessary. However, as a lot of print jobs rely on third-party-supplied materials, it is sometimes unavoidable.

guide to print resolution

Printing requirements are dictated by the final quality and detail required. Posters usually print at a minimum of 100dpi and a maximum of 150dpi. Print jobs such as flyers and brochures print with a minimum resolution of 300dpi, up to 2,400dpi for very high-quality results.

channels

Each digital image contains several different channels that hold information for the different colors of the color space used to produce it.

RGB images

RGB images are made from the red, green and blue additive primaries and have three channels, one for each color. When combined, the channels give a full-color composite image. An image stored as RGB is smaller than a CMYK file because it has one channel fewer. For this reason, RGB images are used on screen because they have the same color space as an RGB screen. They also have the added benefits of being brighter than CMYK images and having smaller file sizes as they contain one channel less.

Composite RGB image.

The three separate channels: red, green and blue.

red channel

blue channel

CMYK images

CMYK images are made from the cyan, magenta, yellow and black subtractive primaries and have four channels, one for each color. When combined, the channels give a full-color composite image. An image stored as CMYK is larger than an RGB file because it has one channel extra. CMYK images are used for printing with the four-color printing process as each channel corresponds to one of the printing plates.

splitting channels

A digital image can be split into its separate channels so that each can be worked on and adjusted individually. This can be done to touch up and make subtle adjustments to a particular color. Splitting channels can also be useful when converting to grayscale, as described later on pages 90—91.

The channels palette allows the user to split the channels.

altering images in CMYK and RGB

Alterations to an image will produce different results depending on the color space used (as they have a different number of channels). As an RGB image has three channels and a CMYK image four, the resulting composites vary. Pictured are examples of an image that has been inverted, equalized and solarized.

However, not all manipulation techniques can be applied to a CMYK image. For example, Photoshop's Glowing Edges command only works on an RGB image, while the Find Edges command produces the same result in both RGB and CMYK modes. As a general rule, keeping the original as an RGB file allows for more controlled image alteration. Once the image is finalized it can then be converted to CMYK for printing.

RGB Glowing Edges

RGB image inverted

RGB image equalized

RGB image solarized

CMYK/RGB Find Edges

CMYK image inverted

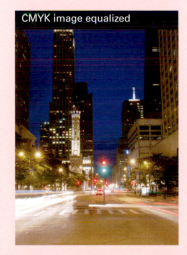
CMYK image equalized

CMYK image solarized

Glowing Edges
This effect applies a neon-like glow to the edges of the image for a dramatic graphic effect. This effect can be applied to images in RGB mode.

Find Edges
This effect creates a drawn border around areas of the image that contain an obvious transition in color. Both RGB and CMYK images can be worked on in this way.

inverted images
This effect inverts the colors in an image, which, given that RGB and CMYK are different color spaces, produces a very different result depending on the color space used by an image. Inverting an image converts the brightness value of each pixel in the channels to the inverse value on the 256-step color-values scale. For example, a pixel in a positive image with a value of five changes to 250.

equalized images
This effect redistributes the brightness values of the pixels in an image so that they more evenly represent the entire range of brightness levels. Values are remapped so that the brightest value represents white and the darkest value represents black, and then distributes intermediate pixel values evenly throughout the grayscale.

solarized images
This effect blends a negative and a positive image to produce a result similar to exposing a photographic print briefly to light during development. Notice how solarization produces a greater loss of detail in the CMYK image. Notice how solarization produces higher intensity bright spots in the RGB color space.

layers and combining images

The concept of using layers has existed in the arts for many years. Modern graphic design uses foreground, midground and background layers to create depth of field, which is not dissimilar to certain approaches to painting and photography, as can be seen in this print advertisement for Kenzo perfume created by Research Studios that features several images combined as layers with varying degrees of opacity. The delicate balance between the layers creates a soft tapestry as the images on different layers interact with one another like a doubly exposed photograph. The design presents a depth of field with the foreground in sharp focus while the background is blurred.

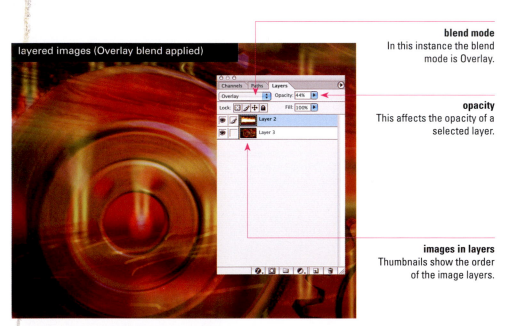

layered images (Overlay blend applied)

blend mode
In this instance the blend mode is Overlay.

opacity
This affects the opacity of a selected layer.

images in layers
Thumbnails show the order of the image layers.

Using layers

Using layers, a designer can work on one element of an image while still being able to view others without disturbing them.

In addition to being able to change the attributes of the layers by applying special filters and blends, just changing their order will alter the visual result. The level of opacity of a layer can also be changed so that it is more or less transparent.

Controlling layer opacity, fill, and blend modes can create multiple effects, as seen on pages 88—89.

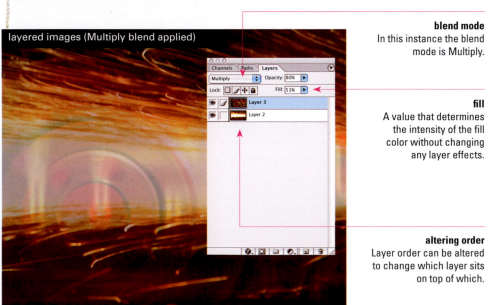

layered images (Multiply blend applied)

blend mode
In this instance the blend mode is Multiply.

fill
A value that determines the intensity of the fill color without changing any layer effects.

altering order
Layer order can be altered to change which layer sits on top of which.

layers and photographic techniques

Layers work like traditional photographic methods, as described below:

double exposure

A technique whereby a negative is exposed, and then intentionally exposed again with a different subject—like two layers overlaying one another.

depth of field

The distance in front of and beyond a subject that is in focus—like one layer in focus, the other not.

cross processing

The method of intentionally developing photographic film using incorrect chemicals—the blend mode can simulate this.

adjustment layers

Adjustment layers allow a designer to alter an image, while preserving the original at the same time. For example, a designer could make alterations to the color levels of a photograph, but if a client subsequently decided that they did not want this alteration, the levels adjustment could easily be turned off to restore the image to its original form. If the levels of the image were changed without an adjustment layer, the designer would have to find the original image file and other alterations such as cleaning the image or color balancing would have to be done again.

original image # 1

original image # 2

combined images

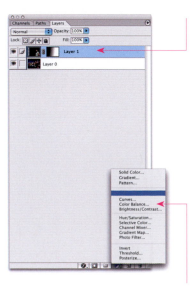

Starting with two original images, a mask can be applied to the top layer (the girl) to combine them (see pages 56—57). When a mask is applied, the black areas of the mask allow the image below to show through, while the white areas block image show-through.

Adjustment layers can then be added to alter each image layer, or the resulting composite image.

gradient map and levels affecting both layers

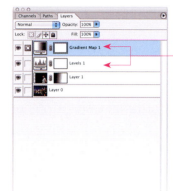

In this first example, the levels in the two images have been altered on one layer to change the brightness of the image and a gradient map has been applied via another. The effect of the two adjustment layers applies to all layers underneath them, which is indicated in the control box by the lack of indentation (see example below).

gradient map affecting both layers, levels affecting layer 1

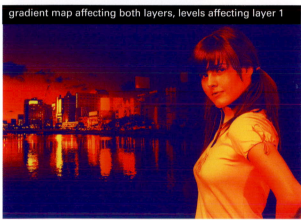

In this example, the image order is the same, but the adjustment layer (levels) only applies to the layer directly below it (the girl) and does not affect the base layer (the cityscape). For this reason it is indented. Holding ALT and clicking the line that divides the layers dictates whether the adjustment layer alters ALL layers below it, or ONLY the layer directly below it.

gradient map and levels affecting layer 1

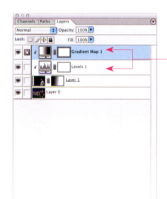

In this example, both the gradient map and the levels adjustment have been set to apply to just the top layer (the girl), leaving the base layer unaltered.

altering gradient map and levels affecting layer 1

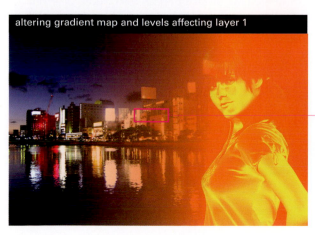

Being able to dictate which layers are affected by the adjustments allows a designer to radically alter one layer while leaving subsequent layers intact.

The mask blends the two images in the middle of the frame. However, if the two images both have a lot of detail in this area the blend may appear uncomfortable. Here this is not an issue as the image of the girl has a solid background that blends easily.

working with clipping paths

A designer often needs to isolate the subject of a photo or one of the elements within an image from its background. This requires the use of clipping paths: paths around an object that clip or omit areas of an image while leaving the original image intact. Here we see how paths can be used to cut out image elements, and how they can be used with adjustment layers to create graphic effects.

isolated image

clipping path

with background color altered

the basic path

Images obtained from image libraries, such as the sunflower above, often include clipping paths so that the subject can easily be isolated from its background. The middle image shows a clipping path around the edges of the sunflower. The clipping path is a series of points and paths drawn as Bézier curves that allow them to conform to the smooth and sharp points of the outline, as illustrated above as a magenta line.

With the object isolated by the clipping path, its background color can be easily changed, as shown in the image on the right. However, as the Bézier curve is the basic path that isolates an image it can be used to do much more than simply cut out and separate an image from its background. These paths are often used as the starting point for more complex image manipulation.

0.25 pixels

1.25 pixels

tolerances

Designers are able to define the tolerance of a path to create different results. Here, the marble to the far left has a path of 0.25 pixels (the finest tolerance possible). However, this path is a vector (a perfect mathematical circle), which, when converted to a raster file, has become a series of pixels. Where there is a change in path direction, the circle has tried to compensate—resulting in an unwanted bitmap effect. Using a lesser tolerance (left) allows the circle to take an arguably less accurate path, but one that produces a smoother, more pleasing result.

depth of field

In photography, depth of field refers to how much of an image is in focus and it relates to the foreground, middle ground and background. By altering the depth of field of an image, the designer allows different areas of the image to become the visual focal point.

In the image to the right, the focus is on the middle ground. The girl is in focus but the wheat in the foreground is not. Depth of field can be manipulated through the use of clipping paths. By drawing a path around the girl, she can be isolated from the rest of the image. Using an adjustment layer, the illusion of depth of field can be added by inverting the clipping path so that everything but the girl is selected. This allows the background to be adjusted to become the focal point. In this way, the girl's face (below centre) is kept in focus while the background and foreground are blurred, and finally a graphic intervention is made to this image with a gradient map (below right).

original image

altered background

altered foreground

gradient map

the paths palette

Any number of paths can be created, allowing the designer to isolate different areas of an image for manipulation in different ways. Creating a new path allows a designer to select the exact area that is to be worked upon.

The screen shot (right) shows how one image has two paths drawn, isolating the hand and the face. These can then be used to manipulate or preserve parts of the image, effectively allowing the designer to control the "photographic" conditions of the original shot.

Channels Paths Layers

hand

face and hair

multiple paths

Individual paths can be stored in separate layers or later combined into a single element. The two paths here were drawn as a series of Bézier curves, one for the hand area and one for the face area.

Using the "hand" path, the foreground can be preserved, while alterations to the background are made equally using the "face and hair" path to alter the focal point of the image.

masks

Masks function in a way that is similar to the gel used by photographers to change the amount of light recorded in a photograph. The following pages will explain how to use masks and layers to combine two original images. Masks allow images to be subtly blended while preserving the information contained in any original images. Fully preserving both images in their original format makes it easier to make subsequent alterations without needing to start again from scratch.

original image #1

original image #2

thinking in black and white

The two original images above are full-color images, but the key rule for using masks is to think in monotone, in other words in black and white. This is necessary as everything in the mask that is black will not show, while everything that is white will. As the original images are in color, this may take some getting used to, but with practice, a designer gets a feel for how different images need to be treated.

mask

The example below shows the two images and the mask, which appears red for illustrative purposes.

The mask is a gradient from black to white, left to right. Where it is black, the image is obscured and where it is white, the image shows through. The opposite page shows how the mask can be altered to allow more or less of the masked street image to blend with the image of the woman's face.

mask

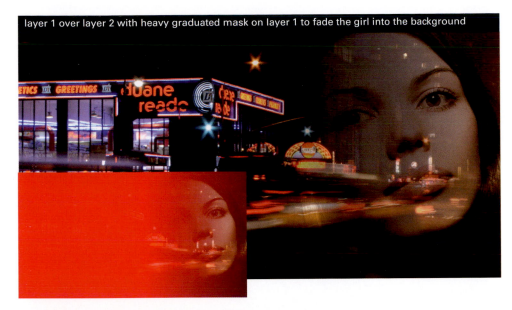

layer 1 over layer 2 with heavy graduated mask on layer 1 to fade the girl into the background

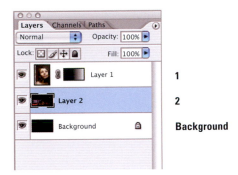

This first image has layer 1 (girl) over layer 2 (street) with a heavy graduated mask on layer 1 to fade the girl into the background and give plenty of show-through to layer 2. Notice how the graduation is black to white, which is why a designer needs to think in monotone.

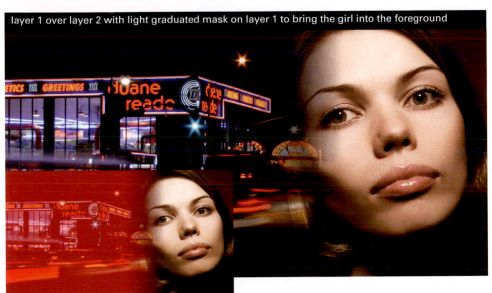

layer 1 over layer 2 with light graduated mask on layer 1 to bring the girl into the foreground

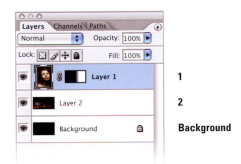

This image shows layer 1 (girl) over layer 2 (street) with a light graduated mask on layer 1 to bring the girl into the foreground, with very little show-through to layer 2.

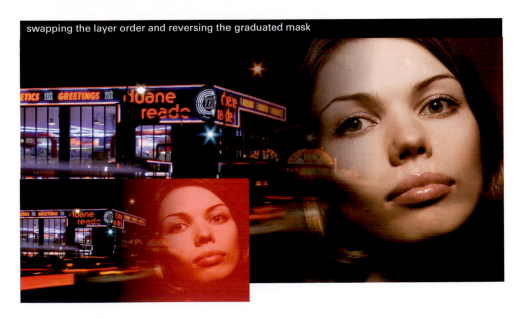

swapping the layer order and reversing the graduated mask

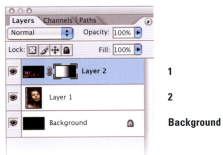

This image achieves the same effect as above, but by swapping the layer order and reversing the graduated mask. Here, layer 2 (street) is over layer 1 (girl), with a graduated mask on layer 2 to block out the street and allow the girl to show through.

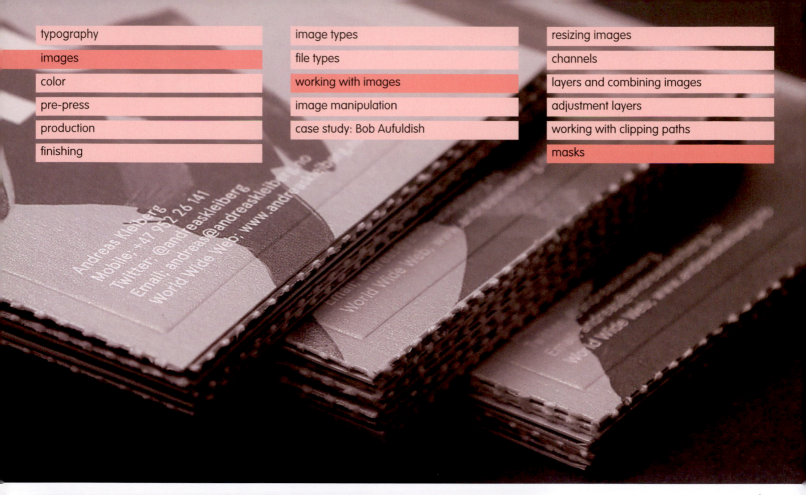

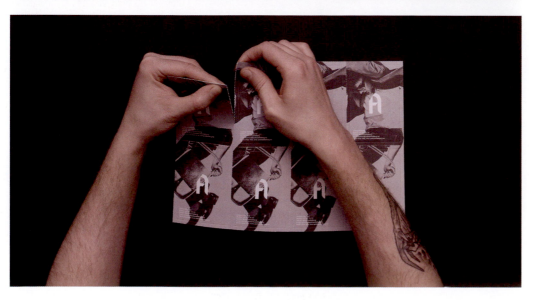

Kleiberg
Pictured are elements created by Norwegian agency Bleed for a new identity for photographer Andreas Kleiberg that uses a reduced color palette of black and white tones to create a sense of understated style and control, and that also provides for constant presentation of the photographer's images.

"Nuit Blanche" (facing page)
Pictured are brochure spreads created by Research Studios for the contemporary art exhibition Nuit Blanche in Paris, France.

The brochure layout is based on the six districts over which the exhibition was presented, using photographs by Stanislas Wolff. The designs were created using masks to isolate and highlight image elements, creating vignettes set against a black background.

This method allows the seamless integration of text and image to form a composite image. Placing the text and image in fluid spaces forms a composite balance of light and color.

BERCY-TOLBIAC

AUTOUR DE PARIS

LE MARAIS

AUTRES QUARTIERS

CARPENTIER

CHAMPS-ELYSEES CONCORDE

LA GOUTTE D'OR

BEAUGRENELLE

image manipulation

Image manipulation is the process through which the visual appearance of an original image is altered. These techniques can be used to produce a wide range of effects, from subtle changes and corrections to more dramatic interventions.

altering images and filters

Filters can be applied to a base image to alter its appearance in many different ways. A designer might use filters to apply an effect to or enhance an image, or to simulate a technique from another discipline as shown opposite. Filters offer powerful options for making images more unique and dramatic, but they need to be used with care and a certain restraint in order to produce a result that is recognizable. The examples shown opposite illustrate the results that can be achieved with filters, whether subtle or ambitious.

Tate Modern (right)
Pictured is a bag created by NB: Studio for the shop of London's Tate Modern. It features images that have been manipulated with filters to obscure their detail, thus visually portraying the atmospheric calm of the gallery. This use of a filter produces a result that is subtle, uncontrived and unselfconscious.

original image

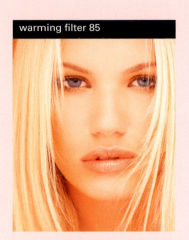
warming filter 85

cooling filter 82

violet

photographic filters (above)
Filters can be used to change the color temperature of an image. They can add warmer tones such as red and yellow (as with warming filter 85), or cooler tones such as blue (as with cooling filter 82), or for a more subtle effect, the violet filter.

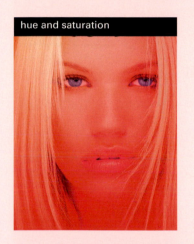
hue and saturation

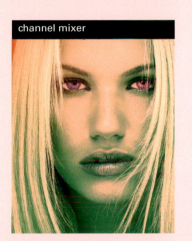
channel mixer

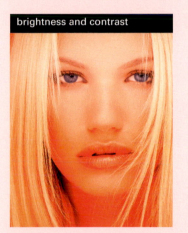
brightness and contrast

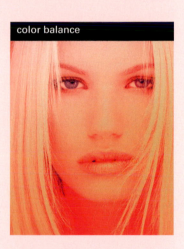
color balance

color alteration filters (above)
Filters can be used to make more graphic interventions, such as that achieved by the channel mixer above, and others that simply adjust color performance.

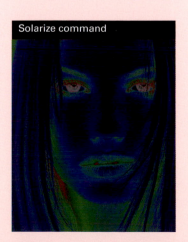
Solarize command

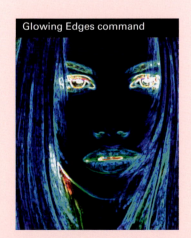
Glowing Edges command

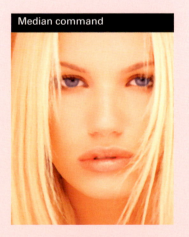
Median command

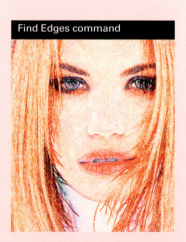
Find Edges command

filters of graphic intervention (above)
Graphic intervention filters implement more radical changes to the image, distorting the colors to create negative images and neon effects, such as with the Solarize and Glowing Edges filters, or more subtle distortions using the original colors, such as with the Median or Find Edges filters.

parallax and transformations

Images can be distorted and transformed deliberately, but sometimes these effects can occur naturally. Parallax, for instance, makes an object appear to be displaced when seen from two different viewpoints and is particularly common in close-up photography. Perspective can cause the distortion problem of converging verticals when photographing tall buildings.

original image

corrected image

An original image in which perspective causes a problem with converging verticals can be corrected, such as is the case with this photo of Times Square in New York City.

Correction of the converging verticals problem is achieved by stretching the top two points of an image element out and to the sides, thus making the top of the building appear wider. This correction is easily noticeable when comparing different elements from the periphery of the corrected image with those in the original, such as the lamp post.

bounding box

All digital images exist within a bounding box, which is a square or rectangle comprising rows of pixels containing image information that can be thought of as a canvas.
Because this canvas is determined by the image pixels, it is always a square or rectangle. The bounding box has corners and mid-points called anchors, which can be pulled or stretched to distort the image. Even if an image such as the light bulb (right) appears to have an irregular shape, it in fact is a square with white pixels.

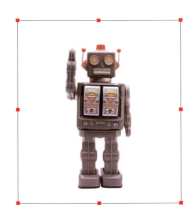

original image
The original image is square-on and contained within a bounding box that has adjustment anchors.

skew
Here, the image has been skewed by slanting its bounding box.

distort
Distort stretches the image bounding box.

perspective
A vertical stretch can be applied to the bounding box to add perspective.

practical application

In practical terms, a combination of the skew, perspective and distort functions allows the accurate removal of distortion where correction is needed, and the distortion of graphic elements that are to be added to an image that has perspective. As an original image will normally contain perspective, any new elements will need to be altered accordingly.

Combining the use of the skew, perspective and distort functions rather than using one alone gives a more realistic and natural-looking visual result. Shown below is a basic example of this. Replacing the images in the frames requires altering each individual image's perspective through a combination of transformation effects.

original image

composite image

case study:

exhibition catalogs
Bob Aufuldish, USA

Positioning images in a publication may seem like a simple proposition, but it can be the deciding factor in the overall effect of a job. Though seemingly simple, getting an image on a page can often be quite complex.

This case study looks at two pieces of work by American designer Bob Aufuldish. The first is an artist's monograph for Lazar Khidekel, and the second is an exhibition catalog for "Overthrown: Clay Without Limits". Both projects highlight how the reproduction of images can make or break a publication, particularly when featuring works of art that require accurate color correction and printing to reproduce the images well.

Good color reproduction starts with having good files to work with. For an exhibition catalog, these will likely be supplied by the institution that commissions the job. Seeing the original artworks can prove invaluable both to color proofing but also to get a feel for them and the impact they have when you look at them. "For the Lazar Khidekel book … knowing the dimensions of the works before I began designing the plates (was important). Because of the difficult economic circumstances under which Khidekel worked at the beginning of his career, many of the works are incredibly small—there is one work that is literally the size of a postage stamp—so I was able to make the works actual size in the book. And because the works were so small many of them were able to be scanned directly, allowing us to reproduce the subtleties of the texture of the paper. We also silhouetted or outlined many of the works in order to emphasize their nature as objects," Bob said.

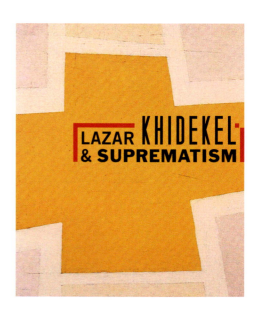

Artist's monograph for Lazar Khidekel (above and facing page)
Images of the artist's work are central to the design of both the cover and spreads of the publication.

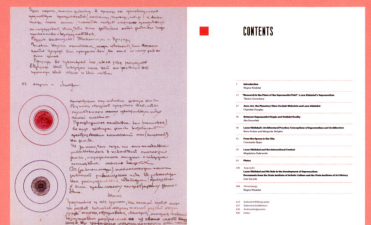

LAZAR **KHIDEKEL**
& SUPREMATISM

CONTENTS

LAZAR KHIDEKEL'S ARCHITECTURAL PRACTICE:
CONCEPTIONS OF SUPREMATISM AND ARCHITECTURE

LAZAR KHIDEKEL AND THE INTERNATIONAL CONTEXT

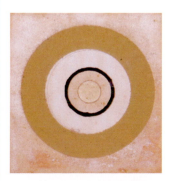

The two-volume "Overthrown" catalog shows how the quality of the raw material images can both limit and provide opportunities for a designer. "For the first volume, which gives background information on each artist, the image files came from the artists or their galleries and the quality varied widely. In a few situations, I was faced with designing based on file size rather than what I thought would work best. However, for the second volume, which documented the site-specific installations at the Denver Art Museum, everything was photographed by the museum's capable staff photographer. He was able to light the installations to show them at their best and photograph from a number of angles. To add to the narrative richness of the catalog, he photographed the artists at work, so the finished and in-process artworks are juxtaposed," said Aufuldish.

While various production techniques are available to a designer, Aufuldish believes that showing artworks as they are has to be the priority. The nuances of the artwork must be taken into account though. As "Overthrown" was about contemporary ceramics, the curator was extremely conscious of not making stereotypical visual references to clay. As the artists use all sorts of techniques, it made sense to introduce a different kind of material—silk screened frosted plastic—for the slipcase, while the volumes of the catalog were more conventional: perfect bound and matt laminated with a spot gloss UV on the cover; CMYK and varnish on the interior. "First and foremost the book must work as ink on paper—ink defining the typography and the imagery; the paper determining the way the book feels in your hands and on the tips of your fingers, and the way the unprinted areas are activated as negative space. All these must be in service to the content," he said.

Slipcase for the "Overthrown" catalog
Pictured below is a detail of the silk screened frosted plastic slip cover for Overthrown; far removed from the ceramic subject matter.

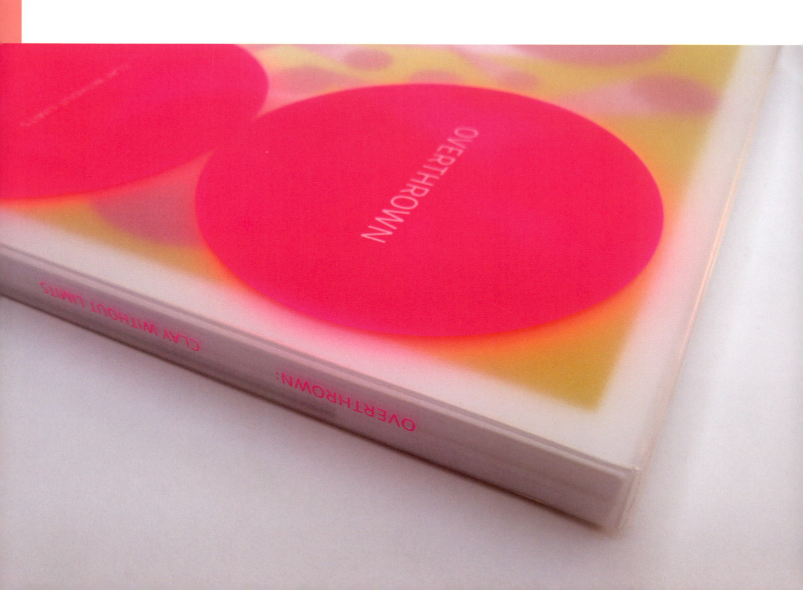

Production and printing techniques are typically used help to help present artworks in catalogs to their best effect. However, the production can be an intrinsic part of the resulting piece. The contemporary music score Explorer Producer Stoic After Your Fashion designed by Aufuldish with composer Bill Smith.

The book block was cut into sections so that the spreads effectively became like exquisite corpses that could be reconfigured by each performing musician to collide and juxtapose different images, as shown above. The score including several reader's ribbon so that the musicians could mark their choices. A hole was drilled into the front of the book block to house a dice, which was a necessary part of determining what the musicians were to play. A plastic sheet in a pocket in the back of the score was used by the musicians to crop the spreads they'd chosen. "Scores of contemporary music don't necessarily use the standard staff and notes that we're used to. … All of this manipulation happens on stage and in itself is part of the performance. In this situation, all the materials and production techniques are absolutely intrinsic—without any one of them the score would not be able to be performed," he said.

Music score for Explorer Producer Stoic After your Fashion
Rather than using a traditional staff and notes, this score is cut into three sections so that it can be reconfigured by each performing musician.

"First and foremost [a] book must work as ink on paper— ink defining the typography and the imagery; the paper determining the way the book feels in your hands and on the tips of your fingers, and the way the unprinted areas are activated as negative space."

chapter three

color

Color has become a permanent fixture in the field of visual communication as magazine and newspaper producers have taken advantage of four-color printing technology developments. The emergence of affordable color printing technologies has also meant that small companies and homes can produce color documents quickly and cheaply.

Color adds dynamism to a design, attracting the attention of the viewer, and perhaps eliciting an emotional response. Color can also be used by a designer to help organize the elements on a page and lead the eye from one item to another, or to instill hierarchy.

Printing technology continues to expand the boundaries of color reproduction, as developments such as six-color hexachromatic printing push the color gamut to new dimensions.

X-rummet
Pictured are exhibition catalogs created by Danish design agency Designbolaget for the National Gallery of Denmark's experimental stage for contemporary art. They feature an identity comprised of six Xs executed with different types of lines but within the same dimensions, each one representing one artist's participation. Each brochure has a simple color intervention of a pantone base color overprinted with black on an uncoated stock that provides a consistent identity, even though the artists' works are very different.

basic terminology

A great deal of terminology is used to describe color and its various functions. This spread examines those that are used to help designers, photographers, artists, printers and other professionals communicate color ideas.

describing color

As color is essentially different wavelengths of light, design and color professionals use different values of hue, saturation and brightness to describe it. Importantly for designers, there are two main color models, as illustrated below, that relate to work on screen (RGB), and printed work (CMYK).

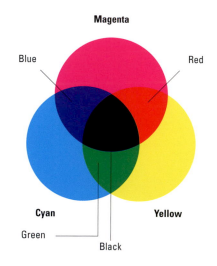

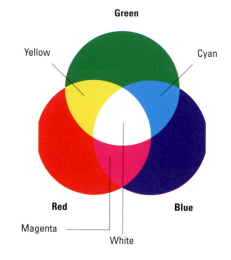

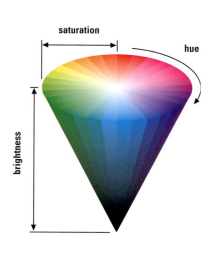

CMYK (Cyan, Magenta, Yellow and Black)
This diagram shows the subtractive primary colors. Each of these has one of the additive primaries missing. Where two subtractive primaries overlap, only one additive primary is visible. Blue is formed where cyan and magenta overlap. Cyan and yellow overlap to produce green. Magenta and yellow combine to form red. Where all three subtractive colors overlap, black is produced because no light escapes.

RGB (Red, Green and Blue)
This diagram shows the additive primaries. Where red and green overlap, yellow is created. Magenta is formed where red and blue overlap, and cyan is created where blue and green overlap. These secondary colors are the subtractive primaries. Each additive primary represents a component of white light, so where all colors overlap, white is produced.

brightness, hue and saturation
These terms help a designer to specify and communicate color information and help overcome the potential vagaries of computer screens and printing presses where a color is not always what it seems. Accurate color description in terms of the hue, saturation and brightness helps a designer and printer meet the expectations of a client.

alternative names for describing color

value

Value is another way of referring to brightness: how light or dark a color is.

chroma

Chroma is another way of referring to hue, the colors formed by different wavelengths of light.

brightness, hue and saturation in practice

Hue, saturation and brightness are the three color elements that can be manipulated to change the appearance of an image. Color manipulation of images is now relatively straightforward through the use of image-editing software, which allows a designer to easily alter the feel of a photo, as well as correct color problems.

hue

Changing the hue of an image changes its color. In the duotone example above, the hue changes from magenta to black. Altering the hue changes the color but leaves the saturation and brightness at their original levels.

saturation

In this example, saturation—the purity of the color—changes from none (left) to full (right), which gives a hyper-real result. In this instance, the brightness and hue are the same, but the change in saturation produces an intense change.

brightness

Brightness can be changed by mixing an image with black or white. Here, the image changes from a black mix (left) to a white mix (right) with the base image in the middle. Here, the hue and saturation remain unchanged, but the image appears faded or masked, with high or low levels of brightness.

neutral gray

The background color of this page is neutral gray, a color that is used to allow a designer to more accurately see the balance of colors in an image by providing a neutral base contract. Neutral gray is made from 50 per cent cyan, 40 per cent magenta and 40 per cent yellow, which in the RGB colour space is 128 red, 128 green and 128 blue.

color management

Color management is a process that governs how color is translated from one piece of equipment in the printing process to another. Color management is needed to ensure accurate and predictable color reproduction because each device responds to or produces color differently.

gamut and color space

Gamuts and color spaces are used by designers and printers to calculate the range of colors that can be produced with a given set of colorants on a particular device or system.

gamut

In the printing industry the common gamuts are RGB, CMYK and, more recently, hexachrome, which has a six-colour gamut of CMYKOG (orange and green). The range of spectral colours visible to the human eye can also be described as a gamut and is represented by the bell-shaped image below.

Color printing systems cannot reproduce the full spectral color gamut that the human eye can see. The RGB gamut can reproduce about 70 per cent of these colors and the CMYK gamut reproduces even fewer than this. A designer needs to be aware of these limitations when using the standard four-color printing system in order to avoid the use of colors that cannot be printed. When a color is outside of the CMYK gamut it is substituted for a best-guess replacement that may be noticeably different.

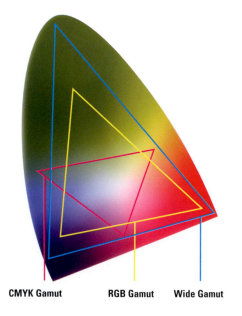

CMYK Gamut   **RGB Gamut**   **Wide Gamut**

common color spaces

RGB

The RGB color space can reproduce about 70 per cent of the colors in the spectral gamut that can be perceived by the human eye.

sRGB

Standard RGB is a standard, device-independent, calibrated color space defined by HP and Microsoft in the 1990s to provide a consistent way to display color internet images on computer screens (CRTs).

ColorMatch RGB

ColorMatch RGB has a wider color space than sRGB and was developed to closely simulate CMYK press work. ColorMatch RGB features a lower gamma than that of sRGB. Gamma affects how bright mid-tones appear and so switching to ColorMatch RGB can be a simple way to brighten a photo.

RGB

sRGB

A color is made up of different quantities of red, green and blue light, given as a ratio such as 88/249/17. These ratios produce different results in different color spaces, as can be seen in the two green panels (left), which use the RGB and sRGB color spaces.

In order to have accurate and reliable color reproduction it is necessary to know how different devices in the design and print production system use color. Although devices may use color in different ways, the International Color Consortium has produced a set of profiles to standardize the ways in which devices communicate color information.

color space

Each device used in the graphic design and printing industries produces or reproduces a certain array of colors called a color space. For example, RGB is the additive primary color space that computer monitors use and CMYK is the subtractive primary color space used in the four-color printing process. Digital cameras, scanners and printers all have color spaces. Each color space reproduces a limited amount of colors within the overall spectral color gamut, in other words the colors that the human eye can perceive.

A digital camera records light as pixels and each pixel records red, green or blue light values. The color space provides a definition for the numeric value of this combination of colors present in a pixel, with each value representing a different color. Changing the color space will change the color associated to this value, which means that, while creating a design or making adjustments to images, it is necessary to be aware of the color space that is being worked in.

Euroscale Coated/Uncoated

SWOP

color profiles

Euroscale Coated is a color profile that uses specifications designed to produce quality separations using the CMYK process. It was created to define CMYK for offset-printing on glossy paper, with colors generated by mixing the four process color inks under the following printing conditions: 350 per cent total area of ink coverage, positive plate and bright white-coated stock.

The Euroscale Uncoated profile is a CMYK working space created for use with uncoated stock under the following printing conditions: 260 per cent total area of ink coverage, positive plate and uncoated white offset stock.

SWOP (specifications for web offset publications) is a standard color profile used to ensure the consistent quality of advertising in publications in North America. Adobe Photoshop uses the SWOP profile as its default for making CMYK color separations.

Pantone and spot colors

Graphic designers use spot colors to ensure that a particular color in a design will print. This may be necessary if the color is outside the range or gamut of possibilities of the four-color CMYK printing process, or because there is a pressing need for a specific color, such as for a corporate logo. Special colors have greater intensity and vibrancy as they print as a solid color rather than one that is composed of half-tone dots, as the panels below show.

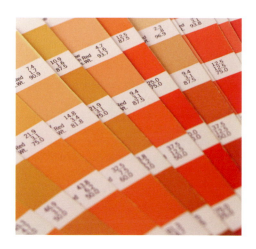

spot colors and CMYK

The centre square above is printed as a fluorescent PM 806 spot color and its nearest CMYK version is printed on the right. The process color square is much duller than the spot color version as it is made with half-tone dots of colour, whereas the special color is applied as a flat color. The approximation of a CMYK color to a process color varies. In this example, the color conversion uses a 50 per cent magenta and no color and so it essentially prints as a tint that lacks the vibrancy of the spot color.

mixing a spot color

Spot colors are made from various base elements, mixed according to a specific recipe. Spot color inks can be bought pre-mixed and ready to use or they can be created by mixing the constituent parts as printers will not stock each individual spot color.

Pantone systems

The Pantone PMS color system has developed to include a wide range of different colors, including special solid, hexachrome, metallic and pastel colors. The Pantone system allocates a unique reference number to each hue and shade to facilitate communication between designers and printers, such as Pantone 806C, the fluorescent spot color used on this page. The 'C' stands for Coated, while other reference letters are 'U' for Uncoated, 'EC' for Euro coated and 'M' for Matt.

Pantone guides explained

Pantone solid

A range of solid metallic, pastel and process colors that can be used on different paper stocks and substrates. The fluorescent above and opposite would be Pantone 806U, 806C or 806M depending upon whether it is to print on matt, coated or uncoated stock.

Pantone pastels

A range of flat, solid, but very pale colours. These are different to tints as they print as a solid color without visible dots. They are available in both coated and uncoated swatches.

Pantone hexachrome

A range of six process colors used for hexachrome printing. In addition to the CMYK process colors, the system adds green and orange process colors allowing it to reproduce 90 per cent of the Pantone PMS colors.

Pantone metallics

A range of over 300 special colors that give a metallic effect including silver, gold and copper colors. Metallics are available in varnished and unvarnished coated swatches.

AMELIA BOARD
Marketing Executive

MTV Networks Australia
p +61 2 8998 9017 m +61 422 199 188
e amelia.board@vimn.com w www.mtv.com.au

REBECCA BATTIES
General Manager, Music & Comedy

MTV Networks Australia
p +61 2 9921 0232 m +61 400 990 044
e rebecca.batties@vimn.com w www.mtv.com.au

MTV Classic
MTV Hits
MTV Live HD
Comedy Central

KIM LANSER
Digital Media Senior Manager

MTV Networks Australia
p +61 2 9921 0229 m +61 408 672 165
e kim.lanser@vimn.com w www.mtv.com.au

JAMES D
EA to G

MTV
p +

MTV Stationery
Pictured are corporate business
cards created by Motherbird for MTV.
Each card features a black-and-white
photo of a member of MTV staff that
is overprinted by a word in a spot
fluorescent ink. This adds a fun feel that
is in line with the brand.

color correction

Photographs often need color correction due to an imperfect or inaccurate assessment of the light when shooting.

basic color adjustment

Many image manipulation programs feature adjustment tools to make automatic color adjustments in order to cope with common problems, such as red eye or color balance problems.

color balance

The color balance command can be used to remove simple color casts by changing the overall color mix in an image. This color correction is performed in relation to the colors within the image. However, by using the techniques explained over the next few pages, designers can exercise more control over color than these simple commands provide.

desaturation

Converting an image from the RGB color space to CMYK will dull its colors because those outside the CMYK gamut suffer distortion (as can be seen below). The lipstick loses its bright red hue while the gold base is less affected. This problem can be avoided using the saturation command. With the image in RGB mode, desaturate it to bring its colors within the CMYK gamut and then convert to CMYK. This will result in an image that is still dull, but more balanced and less distorted.

Using the Color Balance command, a designer can increase or decrease the amount of a color in an image by dragging the sliders relating to each color.

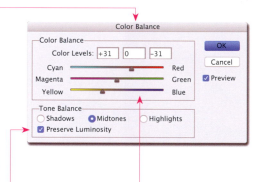

original image / color balanced image

Ticking the Preserve Luminosity box prevents the image's luminosity values changing while the colors are changed, which maintains its tonal balance.

To correct the original image (far left), which has a blue cast, the sliders with blue in them (cyan/red and yellow/blue) have been altered to remove it (left).

RGB image / CMYK image

automated color features

Various automated correction controls allow the designer to perform simple standard adjustments to an image.

original image

auto levels

auto contrast

auto color

This is an image that is to be color corrected.

In this image the auto color command neutralizes mid-tones on its default setting (using RGB 128 gray), and clips shadow and highlight pixels by 0.5%. The default settings can be changed by the designer.

Auto contrast automatically adjusts the contrast and color mixture in an RGB image. This command clips shadow and highlight values and maps the remaining lightest and darkest pixels to pure white (level 255) and pure black (level 0). This makes highlights appear lighter and shadows appear darker.

This command adjusts image contrast and color by neutralizing mid-tones (using RGB 128 gray) and clipping shadow and highlight pixels by 0.5%.

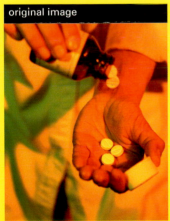

original image

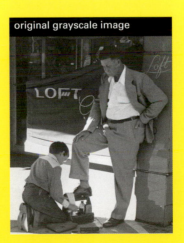

auto levels, contrast and color

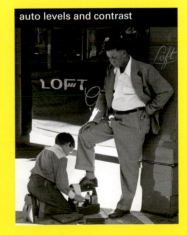

original grayscale image

auto levels and contrast

correcting in color

The original image, above left, appears to be suffering from some distracting yellow and orange color casts. The auto levels, auto contrast and auto color commands can make a good assumption about how to correct the image based on the mid-tones, highlight and shadow areas, which can provide a designer with a good starting point for color correction. However, to obtain a good balance (the corrected image still has a red cast), manual adjustment is usually also necessary.

correcting in grayscale

Although grayscale images contain no color, the auto contrast and auto level commands can still be used to correct an image by calibrating it to a set of reference parameters. However, fine tuning is best done by eye to obtain a natural-looking result as software programs make assumptions during automatic correction and are unaware of the end result the designer is trying to achieve.

variations and selective color

Images can be color corrected or given color intervention through the use of the Variations and Selective Color commands in Adobe Photoshop.

the Variations command

The Variations command allows a designer to adjust image color balance, contrast and saturation while showing thumbnails of the alternatives. This command is useful when an image does not require precise color adjustment, but an overall slanting of the color information in an image.

This simple but effective approach uses a thumbnail of the original image and the adjusted image (current pick) set side by side for direct comparison. The variations of color options are then set in a circle around the 'current pick' image, allowing a designer to see the different color possibilities.

Comparable images
The original image and the changed image are juxtaposed for easy comparison to see the effect the changes are making.

Current Pick
This is the image that is being worked on and it is surrounded by potential color variations, allowing for easy visual comparison.

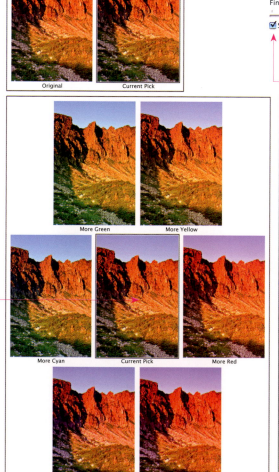

Mode
The Mode box allows a designer to select shadows, mid-tones or highlights according to whether adjustments need to be made in the dark, middle or light areas of an image. The Show Clipping option allows a designer to see which colors will be clipped if they exceed their maximum saturation (see below).

Show Clipping
The Show Clipping option provides a neon preview of areas in the image that will be clipped and converted to pure white or pure black by the adjustment being made. Clipping does not occur when you adjust mid-tones.

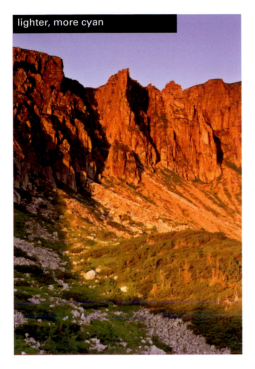

lighter, more cyan

original image

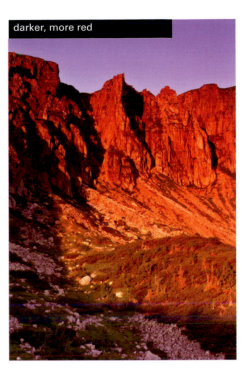

darker, more red

This mountain image has been adjusted and lightened through the addition of cyan. It now has an early morning feel

The original, unadjusted image.

This image has been made darker and has had more red added to warm it, to create the feeling of a sunset.

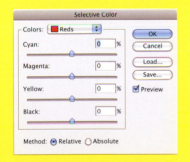

Selective Color

Colors: Reds

Cyan: 0 %
Magenta: 0 %
Yellow: 0 %
Black: 0 %

OK
Cancel
Load...
Save...
Preview

Method: ● Relative ○ Absolute

These controls allow a designer to determine whether selective color is applied relatively or absolutely.

the Selective Color command

The Selective Color command allows a designer to change the colors within a color. Selective color can be applied relatively or absolutely. The relative method changes a color according to the percentage of the total that it represents. For example, adding 10% to a pixel that is 40% cyan adds 4% to it for a total of 44% cyan. The absolute method applies an absolute value to the change so that in this instance, adding 10% to the 40% cyan changes it to 50%.

The original image above has blue in the sky but little in other areas, so it is possible to alter the blue sky without changing the rest of the image. This is done by changing the values of the subtractive primaries on the blue channel (not the cyan channel). Performing selective color correction in this way is based on a table showing the amount of each process ink used to create each primary color. Increasing or decreasing the amount of the process inks in relation to one another means a designer can selectively alter the amount of a process color in any primary color without affecting the other primary colors.

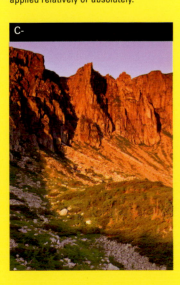

C-

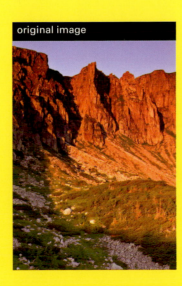

original image

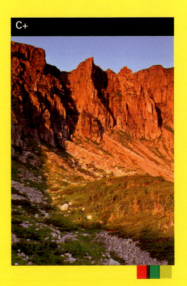

C+

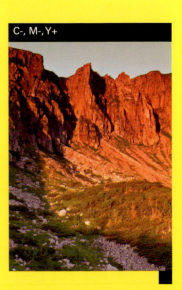

C-, M-, Y+

removing color casts

A color cast exists when the colors in an image are not properly balanced. This typically occurs when a camera's settings are incorrect for the prevailing lighting conditions. A cast can appear across the entire range of pixel values or be limited to the highlight, shadow, or mid-tones of an image.

Color Balance
The Color Balance tool allows color values to be changed between red, green and blue, and cyan, magenta and yellow.

Tone Balance
The Tone Balance tool allows a designer to adjust the shadows, highlights or mid-tones. Most color information is in the mid-tone.

identifying a color cast by eye

It may be difficult to detect an imbalance in the colors by eye alone, perhaps due to the surrounding lighting conditions or the color presentation of the computer screen. However, if you know that an image suffers from a color cast it can often be altered by using a simple color balance application. Where you are unsure if there is a color cast, there are two methods (described opposite) to help identify it.

The Color Balance tool in Photoshop allows a designer to alter shadows, mid-tones and highlights independently of each other and so focuses on specific image areas. In the image below, where there is obviously a green cast, removing some of the green in its highlights balances the image. Most color correction is done in mid-tone areas, as their shadows contain most of the black in an image and their highlights most of the white, meaning that there is normally less to correct here. A photographer will often do this prior to delivering photos to a designer, although this cannot be guaranteed.

image with green color cast

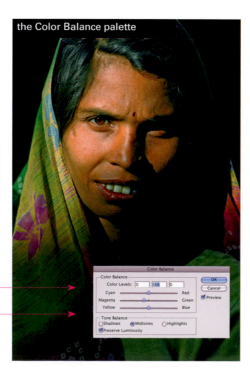

the Color Balance palette

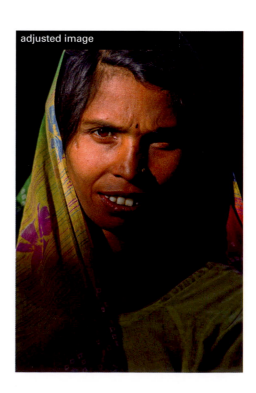

adjusted image

original image with color cast

red channel

green channel

blue channel

identifying a cast using channels

Displaying color channels separately will often reveal color casts. In the example above left there is clearly an extreme green cast. Looking at the individual color channels of this image also confirms this. The red and blue channels are clearly stronger than the green channel, indicating that the image suffers from a green cast.

In the same way, the absence of density in the blue channel would reveal a blue cast, and in the red channel, a red cast. Due to the way that channels work, a reduction in the channel value produces an increase in that color's presence in the image. It is helpful (although this may sound confusing) to think of the channel as a negative—the lighter it is, the more light will flood through, producing a darker image.

image with colour cast

adjusting curves

corrected image

identifying a cast using a color picker

Another method designers use for detecting color casts is to use a color picker and select something in the image that they are certain should be color neutral, such as a sample of a stone on the floor. The color picker here reveals a distinct green tinge. Using the color curves, a designer can select that colour channel and alter it until the image color is adequately corrected.

using curves

A curve is a graph or line along which each point represents a combination of two variables, such as two different colors. Changing the shape of the graph by adding new points allows these variables to be altered to change the color in an image. It is possible to adjust either individual channels or the image as a whole.

color correction using hue

Hue is the color reflected or transmitted from an object, so adjusting the hue of an image in Photoshop is a quick and easy way of altering its color.

altering colour

Color correction can be subtle or dramatic, depending on the need of a design. Using the Hue option allows color alteration without changing the color saturation, luminance or shadows and highlights of the original image. Put simply, if you want to turn a red apple into a green one, this can be easily done by placing a layer of the color you want over the original image, rather like a photographer uses a color gel over the lens.

limitations

The use of hue to correct color has its limitations as all the information in the image is subject to the same degree of color change. This tinting can be avoided by removing sections from the colored layer. Shown below is the colored apple layer with the eaten section and stalk removed, meaning the skin will be altered but the flesh and stalk will remain unchanged.

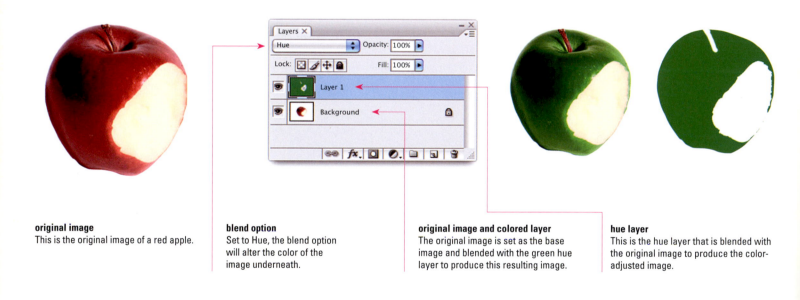

original image
This is the original image of a red apple.

blend option
Set to Hue, the blend option will alter the color of the image underneath.

original image and colored layer
The original image is set as the base image and blended with the green hue layer to produce this resulting image.

hue layer
This is the hue layer that is blended with the original image to produce the color-adjusted image.

The sequence below shows how the hue of an image can be changed or corrected through the use of layers. The original image is changed from red to blue and then green by blending a hue layer with the original image, subtly altering the white areas.

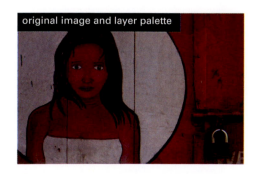
original image and layer palette

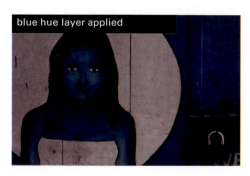
blue hue layer applied

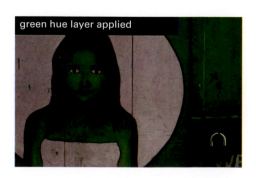
green hue layer applied

Changing the model's hair color is a more subtle example. A layer matching the shape of the model's face was created in order to allow the designer to make adjustments to the model's hair and face independently of each other.

original image

The original, unaltered image.

'hair' layer

Adding a red layer to the background area will affect the hair only.

altered hair #1

Applying a red hue layer over the hair alters the color of the hair only, as the background is white and remains relatively unaltered.

altered hair #2

Adding a gray layer results in the hair becoming a silvery gray color.

warm skin tones

By adding additional hue layers, image elements can be altered independently. Here, the skin tones are warmed.

cool skin tones

Skin tones can also be cooled.

altered eyes and lips

With another adjustment layer, the color of the eyes and lips can be altered.

lightened

Further adjustments can be made to independent layers or the image as a whole.

contrast adjusted

These adjustments can be undertaken until the desired result is achieved.

dodge and burn

Dodge and burn effects are used to lighten or darken areas of an image, and are based on techniques traditionally used by photographers to regulate exposure on specific areas of a print.

dodge

Photographers hold back light when exposing photographic film in order to lighten an area of the print. This is called dodging. Dodging essentially lightens pixels where you paint.

burn

Photographers increase the exposure to light when exposing photographic film to darken areas. This is called burning. Burning essentially darkens pixels where you paint.

color images

When used with color prints or images, dodging and burning gives a designer the ability to alter highlights, mid-tones (where most color information is kept) or shadows. Fortunately these techniques are very forgiving, so if a bit of background is dodged or burned, it will not be too obvious because these tools alter saturation rather than hue.

By preserving the basic color information, subtle alterations to the original images using saturation and brightness can be made with ease. The lightest image areas are affected when focusing on highlights, the darkest areas when working on shadows, and mid-tones when working on mid-tones.

The dodge tool is used to make image areas lighter. In the image above, the hair, eyes, parts of the face and arms, and the background surf have been dodged, as well as the pattern on the t-shirt.

This is the original, unaltered image. Dodge and burn can be used to suppress or highlight areas of the image, to compensate, for example, for poor lighting conditions at the shoot stage.

In this image, areas of the face and hair have been burned to make them darker, essentially increasing their contrast with other elements within the image.

grayscale images

Dodge and burn techniques can also be used with a monotone grayscale image to help accentuate details, as seen in the examples below. The dodged image (top) has more detail in darker areas as it lightens pixels, giving the woman's skin more depth. When the image is burned (bottom), the skin loses detail as pixels are darkened, but more detail is seen in darker areas, such as around the eyes and mouth.

converted images

Converting images from the RGB to CMYK color space dulls colors, making them appear washed out. A dab with the sponge tool while in saturation mode can help brighten them again. When working on an image in RGB mode that will subsequently be converted to CMYK, a designer can keep an eye out for colors that are not within the CMYK gamut and use the sponge tool in desaturate mode to bring them into it. The sponge tool in desaturate mode can also be used to tone down background colors, enabling the foreground to stand out more or to give a colorized appearance.

areas dodged

saturated image (bright)

original image

areas burned

converted image (dull)

creative color

Color provides dynamism to a design, elevating certain elements and attracting attention in a way that can elicit an emotional response in the viewer. Creative color use can achieve this by dramatically changing the appearance of something or someone familiar, as these pages show.

color layers

Layers can be used to overlay color panels on to a base image and these can then be blended in different ways to alter the color of the original image, while leaving the contrast and detail intact.

effects on images
The images opposite and below have had a solid yellow panel applied in order to demonstrate how an image's appearance can be changed through blending.

While a yellow panel has been used here, there are millions of colors that could be applied, as well as variations of opacity, thus giving a vast range of possible subtle combinations.

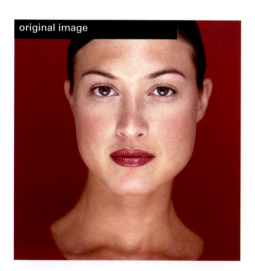

original image

This is the original image to which different effects filters have been applied.

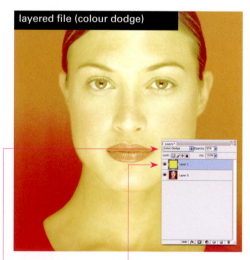

layered file (colour dodge)

blend mode
This control enables a designer to decide how the layer and original image will blend.

colored layer panel
This image blends a color layer with the original image.

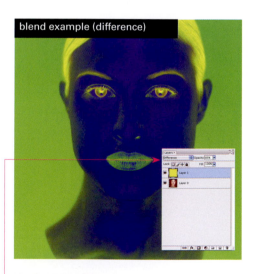

blend example (difference)

blending mode selection
A designer can choose from many different blending modes, such as the difference mode selected here.

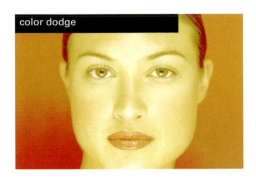

color dodge

The base color in each channel of this image has been brightened to reflect the blend color by reducing the contrast. Blending with black produces no change in a color dodge.

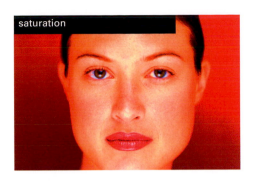

saturation

Saturation produces a color result based on the luminance and hue of the base color and saturation of the blend color. Where there is no saturation in the base image (gray areas), there is no change.

overlay

This effect sees patterns or colors overlaid on to the existing pixels while the base color highlights and shadows are preserved. The base color is mixed with the blend color to reflect the lightness or darkness of the original color.

multiply

With this effect the color intensity of the top layer is multiplied with that of the bottom layer to produce darker colors that give more contrast.

vivid light

The blend color determines if the image is burned or dodged. This lightens lighter than 50% gray or darkens darker than 50% gray.

luminosity

Luminosity produces a color that has the hue and saturation of the base color and the luminance of the blend color.

lighten

Here the lightest base or blend color is selected as the final color, so darker pixels are replaced with the blend color while lighter pixels do not change.

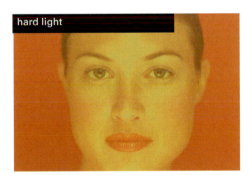

hard light

This effect adds highlights to the image if the blend color is lighter than 50% gray, or adds shadows if it is darker than 50% gray.

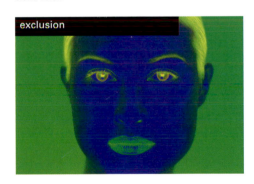

exclusion

The exclusion effect blends the base image with white to invert its color values, producing a lower-contrast version of the Difference effect.

difference

Here the blend color is subtracted from the base color or vice versa depending on which has the greater brightness value, while blending with white inverts base color values.

color

This effect produces colors with the luminance of the base color and the hue and saturation of the blend color, and is used for coloring monochrome and tinting color images as it preserves gray levels.

hard mix

This effect posterizes the base layer pixels through the blend layer and recolors the image by dodging or burning it with a palette of eight colors from the base image.

multiple images

Various blend modes can also be used to merge separate images in Photoshop. Essentially, this is done by combining the colors of the pixels that comprise each image, using the color channels that they are formed with.

original image #1

original image #2

In this example, two images of a face have been used: one serves as the base image upon which the other will be overlaid. The processes highlighted here simulate traditional photography practices like a double exposure or the projection of multiple images on to a wall. The advantage here is the degree of control the user has over being able to alter different facets of one image, such as contrast, while leaving the other image unaffected.

Opacity
The Opacity control determines the extent to which one layer shows through to the next. The greater the opacity, the less the image underneath will show through.

Blend Mode
A designer can select one of many different methods to specify how the different layers blend.

multiple layers
This image is produced with a blend of multiple layers. Each layer can be seen in the command panel.

lighten

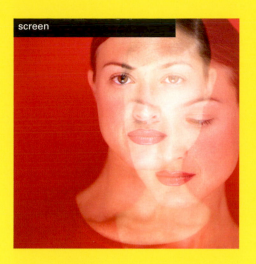

screen

color burn

Images can be merged by working with the color information in each channel in reference to a chosen base color. In this case, the base or blend color will be lighter than the final color and pixels that are darker than this will be replaced. Lighter pixels do not change. The result is a merging of the colors of the images, which become harder to identify on their own.

This process multiplies the inverse of the blend and base colors to produce a lighter color where the images merge. Applying a black screen produces no color change, while screening with white produces white. The result is that while the colors merge, both images can still be clearly identified.

This blend uses a chosen color to colorize the darker pixels of the base image while producing little change to the lighter pixels. This produces a dramatic color intervention in which both images can be identified.

color dodge

difference

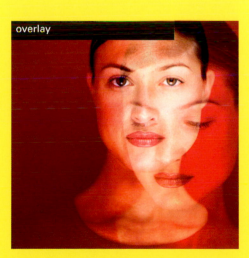

overlay

A color dodge brightens the base color so that it is closer to the blend color, decreases the contrast between the images and helps them to merge so that it is harder to tell them apart.

This process subtracts one color from the other, depending on which of the base or blend colors has the greater brightness value. Blending the result with white inverts the base color values, while a black blend produces no change. The result is that where the images meet, a third visual element is created.

This process overlays patterns or colors on the existing pixels while preserving the highlights and shadows of the base color. In this way the base color is mixed with the blend color to reflect the lightness or darkness of the original color. The result is an image with more intense colors in which both images are identifiable.

grayscale and toned images

Designers can also make graphic interventions to images in order to make them appear to have been shot in grayscale or toned.

original image

colorize box unchecked

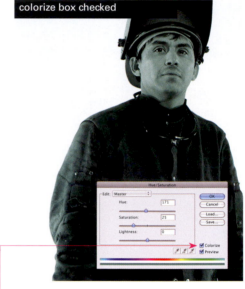

colorize box checked

sepia toning images

To create a sepia-toned image, the hue must be changed before working on the light and dark tonal areas. In the Hue/Saturation dialog box in Photoshop, check the Colorize and Preview boxes and adjust the hue slider to the colour required or enter a value. Then use the saturation slider to determine how much of the hue will be used in the image.

Hue, saturation and lightness are typically used in combination to enhance an image or produce visual effects. The examples below show how altering hue can alter an image's color value while altering the lightness can darken it (center) or lighten it (right).

colorizing

Colorizing is an artistic effect that allows a designer to apply color detail to a selected area of an image. Checking the Colorize box allows the designer to instantly see the effect of any changes made to hue and saturation. Notice the difference between the center (Colorize box unchecked) and right (Colorize box checked) images above.

altered hue #1

image darkened

image lightened

converting images to grayscale

Pictured below is an RGB image that can be converted to create a balanced grayscale image such as the one shown below right. The grayscale image contains one channel (gray), made up of information from the three RGB channels that are shown underneath. Alternatively, a grayscale image can be produced from any of the three RGB channels. As the RGB channels represent sensitivity towards different colored light, each channel has a bias towards the type of light prevalent at different times of the day.

During the early morning, blue light is dominant while red reigns in the evening and green at midday (because neither red or blue are dominant). Externally shot images are generally affected by the sun and so splitting the channels results in three grayscale images with each one being a record of the red, green or blue light. This may give a designer the option, particularly with exterior images, to create an impression of the time of day at which a photograph was shot.

original image

converted to grayscale

blue channel

green channel

red channel

cmyk channels

This image relates to the blue channel of the grayscale image, producing a facsimile of the cool morning light.

This image relates to the green channel of the grayscale image, producing a facsimile of the midday light when neither blue nor red are dominant.

This image relates to the red channel of the grayscale image, producing a facsimile of the warm evening light.

You can also edit color in CMYK mode, which provides for more graphic interpretations of the image.

multi-tones

Duotones, tritones and quadtones are tonal images produced from a monotone original with the use of two-, three- or four-color tones, normally offset against a black base tone.

monotone images

Any multi-tone image begins as a monotone image, such as this one of the Coliseum in Rome, Italy. If an image is not already a monotone, it needs to be converted into one before it can be worked upon in Photoshop.

original image

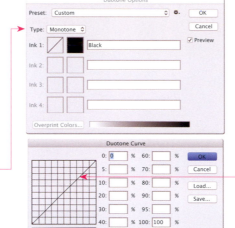

monotone image

Type
The designer chooses whether the resulting image will be mono-, duo-, tri-, or quadtone using one, two, three, or four colors respectively.

duotone curve
Each color in the multi-tone has a curve that can be altered to change its intensity.

duotone images

A duotone image is made of two colors, such as the black and yellow shown below. There needs to be a balanced curve to produce a balanced duotone because if the curve is flattened and pushed to the top it will produce a flooded color, as shown below right.

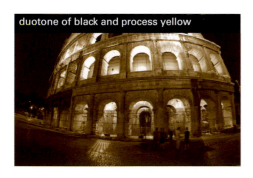
duotone of black and process yellow

duotone with full process yellow

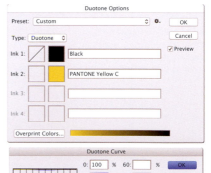

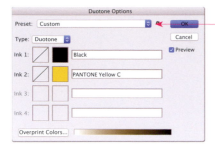

preset values
Preset values can be loaded into the software to remove the guesswork from obtaining good contrast, although trial and error, and experimentation can produce effective results.

altering Duotone Curves
Duotone Curves can be altered to produce subtle or dramatic results. In the examples above, the yellow has been set to run full, flooding the top of the image with color.

tritone images

Adding a third color to a tonal image creates a tritone. The examples below were created using the preset values for the color curves. For example, the middle image simulates a sepia tone and uses magenta, yellow and black, while the image on the right has added depth and color as a result of using certain special colors.

If a multitone image is created using Pantone special colors but is to be printed in CMYK, the image color information needs to be converted to the CMYK color space once it is complete. This will simulate the Pantone colours in the CMYK color space. If a special color is to be used in printing, this can be used in the multi-tone to give a richer color effect.

warm gray preset tritone

sepia preset tritone

Pantone preset tritone

quadtone images

Adding a fourth color creates a quadtone. As with tritones, preset values can be used to create specific effects. The middle image below uses all three subtractive primary colors. Adding a fourth color creates a quadtone. As with tritones, preset values can be used to create specific effects. The middle image uses all four process colors to produce a rich black.

quadtone image

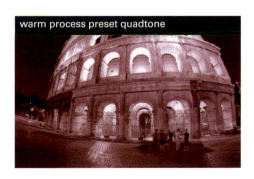

warm process preset quadtone

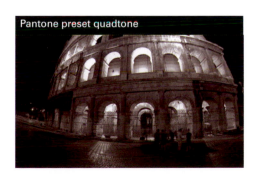

Pantone preset quadtone

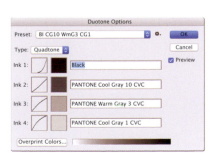

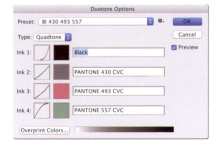

color half-tones

The four-color printing process produces color images from different sized half-tone dots of cyan, magenta, yellow, and black ink, which combine to fool the eye into seeing a continuous-toned image.

original image

color half-tone

using half-tones

Color printing uses separate plates that contain half-tone dots for different printing inks. A designer can manipulate these dots in order to change the appearance of the printed image. Pictured above is an original image, reproduced in the usual way as a continuous-toned image.

Printed here is a graphic interpretation of the same image, but this time using larger half-tone dots to emphasize the fact that it is not actually a continuous tone, but is made up of dots. As can be seen opposite, the composition of these dots is dependent on the mode of the original image—CMYK or RGB.

original image

basic shape with blur applied

half-tone

bordered image

Using half-tones as borders

Half-tone dots can be harnessed to produce different graphic effects such as a creative border on the altered image. Here, a border was created using a simple technique. First, create a shape to be placed over the image, apply blur to it, turn it into a half-tone and use it as a mask to create a graphic border or edge. This can be further controlled by altering the shape and size of the half-tone pattern.

Color Halftone

Max. Radius:	8	(Pixels)	OK
Screen Angles (Degrees):			Cancel
Channel 1:	108		
Channel 2:	162		
Channel 3:	90		
Channel 4:	45		

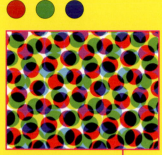

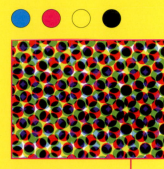

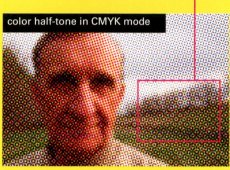

original image

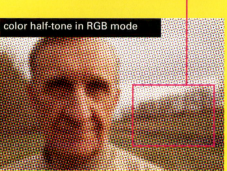

color half-tone in RGB mode

color half-tone in CMYK mode

CMYK, RGB and grayscale

The half-tone dots of each color plate interact to create the impression of a continuous tone because they are aligned at different screen angles. These angles vary depending upon the color mode or color space used. RGB dots replicate those of a computer screen while CMYK dots replicate those used in printing. Any changes to the half-tone dots therefore need to be made in the different color channels of the color space used.

The radius of the dots (their size) and the angles of each color can be altered independently in the dialog box (top left). For grayscale images, only channel 1 should be used. For RGB images, channels 1, 2, and 3, which correspond to the red, green and blue channels are used, and for CMYK images, all four channels, corresponding to the cyan, magenta, yellow, and black channels used.

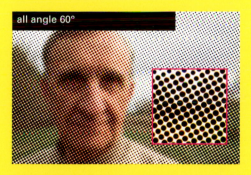

all angle 60°

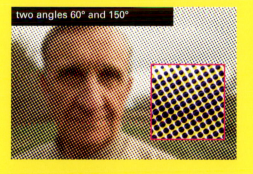

two angles 60° and 150°

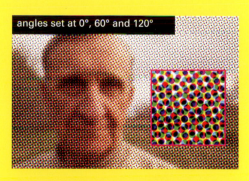

angles set at 0°, 60° and 120°

original grayscale image

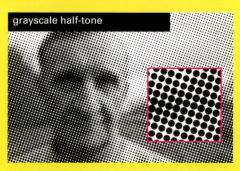

grayscale half-tone

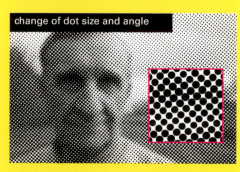

change of dot size and angle

altering screen angles

A designer can control and change the angles and frequency that dots and lines are set at as well as their shape, such as a line, dot, ellipse or square. When the screen angles are not set correctly they interfere and create moiré patterns that disrupt the impression of a continuous tone. Pictured above are images with enlarged details that show how different half-tone angles effect image quality.

Different effects and patterns can be achieved by changing the screen angles (the angle of the dot from the horizontal) relating to the different printing inks. This can be done intentionally to add graphic effect, but be careful not to add a moiré.

color in print

Before sending a design to print, a designer can use a range of methods to ensure that the colors used will appear as intended.

getting the basics right
When work is sent to print, it is unlikely that there will be further opportunities to rectify mistakes. For this reason, it is vital that checks are carried out on some of the most basic elements.

preparing color for print
On completion of the design, the designer must carry out several pre-press checks to ensure clear communication about the job between the designer, client and printer. This is vitally important if the client is to end up with the work that they are expecting. A designer must also review any specific elements that may pose printing problems. The checklist below shows some common color pitfalls when sending files to print. Innovative use of print processes that can help a designer get around the restrictions of a limited budget will also be discussed.

printed pages and panels
Printed pages (or PP) refers to the actual number of pages printed and not the number of sheets printed on. For example, a booklet made from four sheets with print on every side will have eight printed pages once folded. The key is to remember that one sheet printed double-sided is equal to two printed pages. The same rule of thumb applies to the use of panels, which is simply another way of folding a printed sheet.

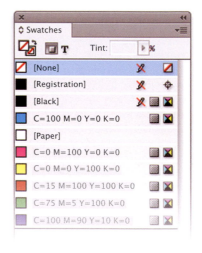

Swatches
This dialog box indicates paper not white, meaning that the item will not be printed but will appear as the same colour as the printing stock.

before sending a file to print:

1 Delete all unused colors.

2 Ensure all that you want to print in black is actually in black, not in registration, as registration will print in all plates.

3 Ensure all that should be in registration is in registration, and not in black, as black will only print on the black plate.

4 Ensure that all spot colors are accounted for. If the job is printing with a special color, all is well; if the job is printing CMYK only, then turn all spot colors to CMYK versions.

5 Ensure all images are converted to CMYK format and not RGB. This includes logos, maps, additional icons, for example. In certain circumstances the printer may prefer the files to be left in RGB for them to convert themselves to match a specific profile, but you can't assume this.

6 Ensure you are clear that your color-fall matches the printer's expectations. If the printer is expecting a four-color job then supplying a file with special spot colors will cause confusion.

7 If the job is being printed on uncoated stock, ensure your imported swatches are of the right value, then set any spot colors as uncoated, and not coated or unspecified.

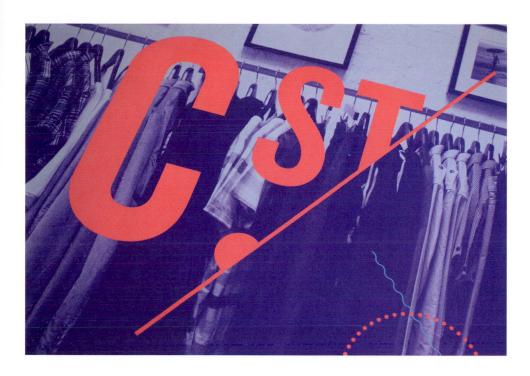

Chapel St
Pictured are elements from a brand identity created by Motherbird for entertainment hub Chapel St Precinct that features a restrained blue colour palette for the majority of the content augmented by sparing use of red elements to add some excitement.

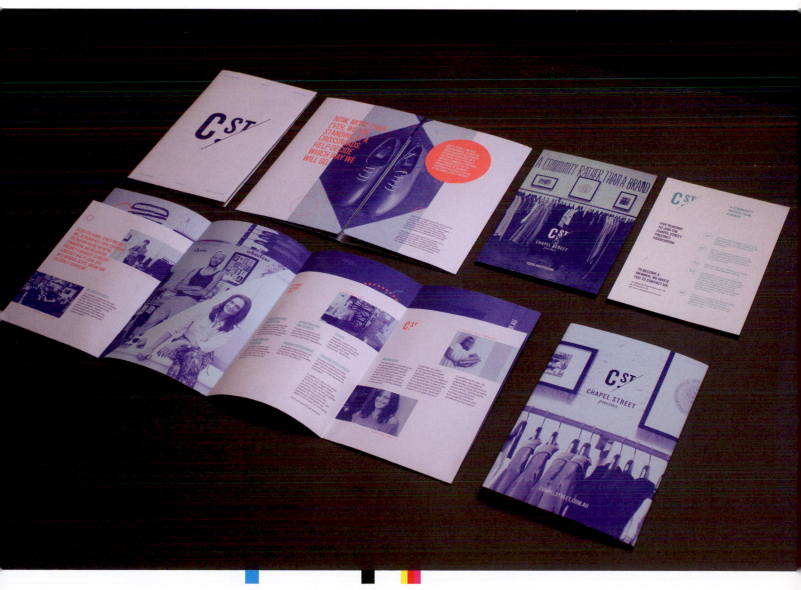

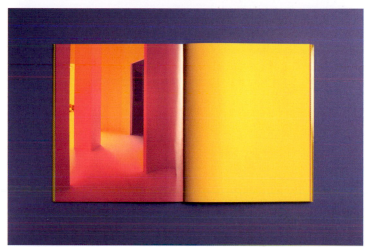

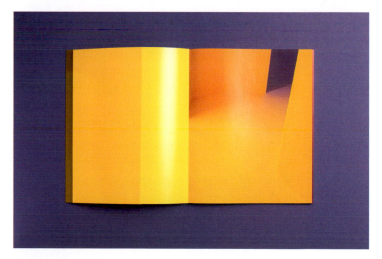

Colour me in
Danish design agency Designbolaget created this brochure for the Colour Me In exhibition at Esbjerg Art Museum. The exhibition spaces were painted in full color, in response to the artworks themselves, and this is reflected in the brochure—the artworks seem to merge and emerge from the pages, much as they did in the physical exhibition. The catalog was printed with process colors on a gloss stock to maximize the color impact, and was contained in a colored acetate cover, with a screenprint of the exhibition title.

tint charts

The chart below shows the 121 tint variations that can be obtained when cyan and black are combined in ten per cent increments. Over 1,000 different tints can be produced by combining the cyan, magenta and yellow process colors together in a similar way as shown in the swatches opposite, with even more variations possible if black is added as well. Over 300 tints can be obtained by combining one of the process colors with black and the same amount again by using single tints of these colors.

These swatches enable a designer to obtain a reasonable idea of the color that will result when combining tints of the different process colors. However, the accuracy of these representations depends upon color control during the printing process, the press used and the stock that a design is printed upon.

Using tints allows a designer to increase the range of color possibilities available when the budget for a job is insufficient to cover the cost of four-color printing. Instead of being limited to the use of two single colors, for example, a designer still has a varied, although limited, color palette available.

As tints are produced using half-tone dots, very light tints such as those of less than ten per cent may not reproduce well, which is why the rule of thumb minimum is ten per cent.

four-color tints of black and cyan

0% cyan 0% black

100% black 0% cyan

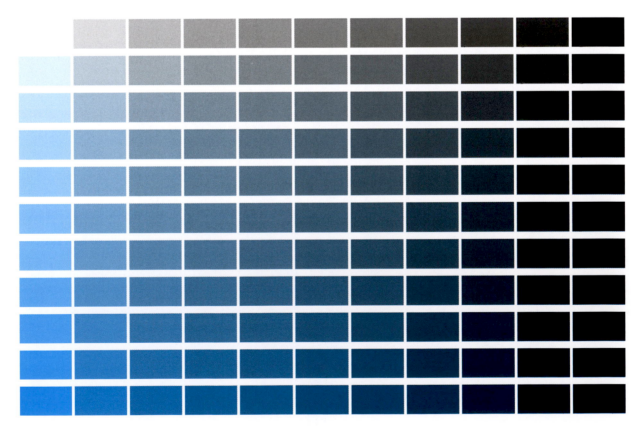

100% cyan 0% black

100% black 100% cyan

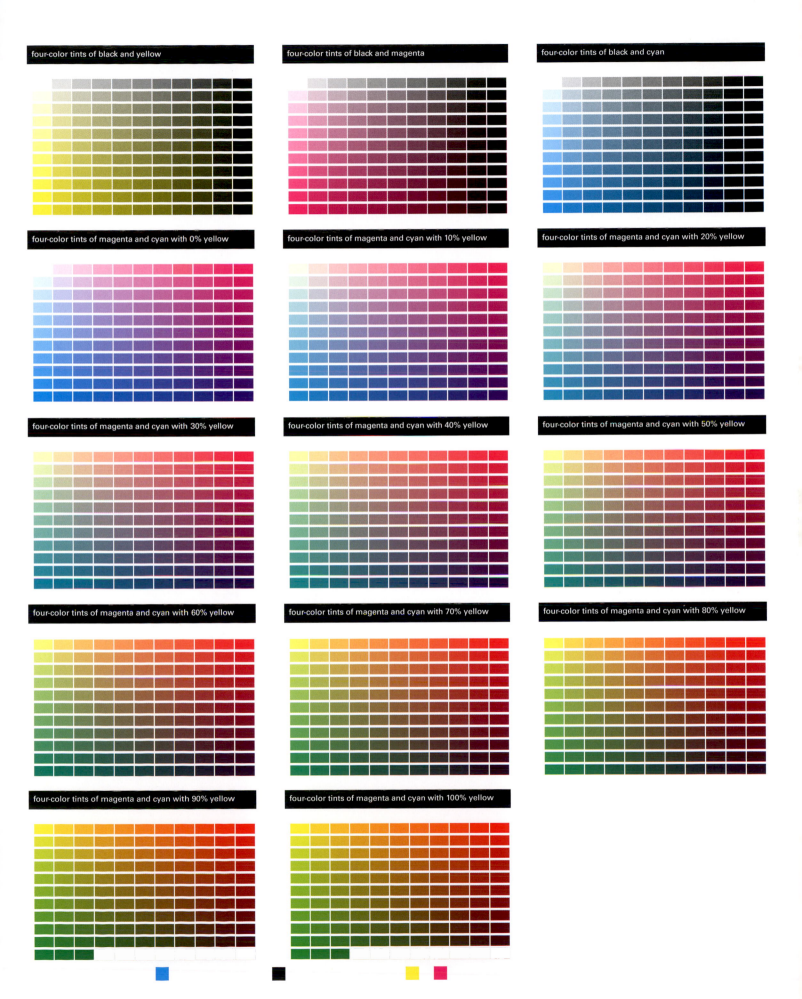

four-color tints of black and yellow

four-color tints of black and magenta

four-color tints of black and cyan

four-color tints of magenta and cyan with 0% yellow

four-color tints of magenta and cyan with 10% yellow

four-color tints of magenta and cyan with 20% yellow

four-color tints of magenta and cyan with 30% yellow

four-color tints of magenta and cyan with 40% yellow

four-color tints of magenta and cyan with 50% yellow

four-color tints of magenta and cyan with 60% yellow

four-color tints of magenta and cyan with 70% yellow

four-color tints of magenta and cyan with 80% yellow

four-color tints of magenta and cyan with 90% yellow

four-color tints of magenta and cyan with 100% yellow

color on screen

On-screen color can be controlled using web-safe colors that ensure consistent color reproduction, regardless of the screen a web page is being viewed upon.

web-safe colors

Web-safe colors are a group of 216 colours, considered to be safe for use in the design of web pages. This palette came into being when computer monitors were only able to display 256 colours and were chosen to match the color palettes of leading web browsers of the time. The web-safe color palette allows for the production of six shades of red, green and blue. This palette has the highest number of distinct colors, within which each color can be distinguished individually.

generating colors in HTML (hex triplet)

Colors are represented in HTML using a hex triplet, which is a six-digit, three-byte hexadecimal number. Each byte refers to either red, green or blue (in that order) with a range of 00 to FF (hexadecimal notation) or 0 to 255 (decimal notation).

For example, producing all three colors at full value results in white, while producing all colors at a level of zero results in black. On-screen colors behave in this way due to their values of light. When all are on they produce white, all off and they produce black, and variants in between produce colors.

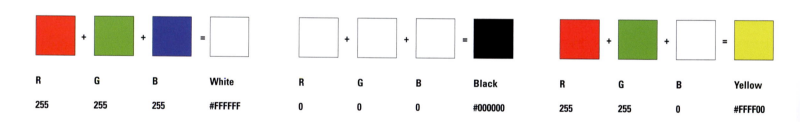

| R | G | B | White | R | G | B | Black | R | G | B | Yellow |
| 255 | 255 | 255 | #FFFFFF | 0 | 0 | 0 | #000000 | 255 | 255 | 0 | #FFFF00 |

HTML colour names

The HTML color palette includes 16 named colors that are pictured below together with their hex triplet notations. This provides a very basic color palette that can be recognized and used by any web browser on any screen. These colors may be specified by name in some applications, and their names are case-independent.

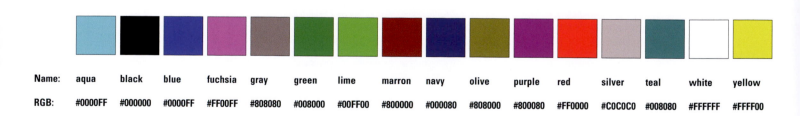

| Name: | aqua | black | blue | fuchsia | gray | green | lime | marron | navy | olive | purple | red | silver | teal | white | yellow |
| RGB: | #0000FF | #000000 | #0000FF | #FF00FF | #808080 | #008000 | #00FF00 | #800000 | #000080 | #808000 | #800080 | #FF0000 | #C0C0C0 | #008080 | #FFFFFF | #FFFF00 |

red colors

IndianRed	CD 5C 5C	205 92 92
LightCoral	F0 80 80	240 128 128
Salmon	FA 80 72	250 128 114
DarkSalmon	E9 96 7A	233 150 122
LightSalmon	FF A0 7A	255 160 122
Crimson	DC 14 3C	220 20 60
Red	FF 00 00	255 0 0
FireBrick	B2 22 22	178 34 34
Darkred	8B 00 00	139 0 0

pink colors

Pink	FF C0 CB	255 192 203
LightPink	FF B6 C1	255 182 193
HotPink	FF 69 B4	255 105 180
DeepPink	FF 14 93	255 20 147
MediumVioletRed	C7 15 85	199 21 133
PaleVioletRed	DB 70 93	219 112 147

orange colors

LightSalmon	FF A0 7A	255 160 122
Coral	FF 7F 50	255 127 80
Tomato	FF 63 47	255 99 71
OrangeRed	FF 45 00	255 69 0
DarkOrange	FF 8C 00	255 140 0
Orange	FF A5 00	255 165 0

yellow colors

Gold	FF D7 00	255 215 0
Yellow	FF FF 00	255 255 0
LightYellow	FF FF E0	255 255 224
LemonChiffon	FF FA CD	255 250 205
LightGoldenrodYellow	FA FA D2	250 250 210
PapayaWhip	FF EF D5	255 239 213
Moccasin	FF E4 B5	255 228 181
PeachPuff	FF DA B9	255 218 185
PaleGoldenrod	EE E8 AA	238 232 170
Khaki	F0 E6 8C	240 230 140
DarkKhaki	BD B7 6B	189 183 107

purple colors

Lavender	E6 E6 FA	230 230 250
Thistle	D8 BF D8	216 191 216
Plum	DD A0 DD	221 160 221
Violet	EE 82 EE	238 130 238
Orchid	DA 70 D6	218 112 214
Fuchsia	FF 00 FF	255 0 255
Magenta	FF 00 FF	255 0 255
MediumOrchid	BA 55 D3	186 85 211
MediumPurple	93 70 DB	147 112 219
BlueViolet	8A 2B E2	138 43 226
DarkViolet	94 00 D3	148 0 211
DarkOrchid	99 32 CC	153 50 204
DarkMagenta	8B 00 8B	139 0 139
Purple	80 00 80	128 0 128
Indigo	4B 00 82	75 0 130
SlateBlue	6A 5A CD	106 90 205
DarkSlateBlue	48 3D 8B	72 61 139

green colors

GreenYellow	AD FF 2F	173 255 47
Chartreuse	7F FF 00	127 255 0
LawnGreen	7C FC 00	124 252 0
Lime	00 FF 00	0 255 0
LimeGreen	32 CD 32	50 205 50
PaleGreen	98 FB 98	152 251 152
LightGreen	90 EE 90	144 238 144
MediumSpringGreen	00 FA 9A	0 250 154
SpringGreen	00 FF 7F	0 255 127
MediumSeaGreen	3C B3 71	60 179 113
SeaGreen	2E 8B 57	46 139 87
ForestGreen	22 8B 22	34 139 34
Green	00 80 00	0 128 0
DarkGreen	00 64 00	0 100 0
YellowGreen	9A CD 32	154 205 50
OliveDrab	6B 8E 23	107 142 35
Olive	80 80 00	128 128 0
DarkOliveGreen	55 6B 2F	85 107 47
MediumAquamarine	66 CD AA	102 205 170
DarkSeaGreen	8F BC 8F	143 188 143
LightSeaGreen	20 B2 AA	32 178 170
DarkCyan	00 8B 8B	0 139 139
Teal	00 80 80	0 128 128

blue colors

Aqua	00 FF FF	0 255 255
Cyan	00 FF FF	0 255 255
LightCyan	E0 FF FF	224 255 255
PaleTurquoise	AF EE EE	175 238 238
Aquamarine	7F FF D4	127 255 212
Turquoise	40 E0 D0	64 224 208
MediumTurquoise	48 D1 CC	72 209 204
DarkTurquoise	00 CE D1	0 206 209
CadetBlue	5F 9E A0	95 158 160
SteelBlue	46 82 B4	70 130 180
LightSteelBlue	B0 C4 DE	176 196 222
PowderBlue	B0 E0 E6	176 224 230
LightBlue	AD D8 E6	173 216 230
SkyBlue	87 CE EB	135 206 235
LightSkyBlue	87 CE FA	135 206 250
DeepSkyBlue	00 BF FF	0 191 255
DodgerBlue	1E 90 FF	30 144 255
CornflowerBlue	64 95 ED	100 149 237
MediumSlateBlue	7B 68 EE	123 104 238
RoyalBlue	41 69 E1	65 105 225
Blue	00 00 FF	0 0 255
MediumBlue	00 00 CD	0 0 205
DarkBlue	00 00 8B	0 0 139
Navy	00 00 80	0 0 128
MidnightBlue	19 19 70	25 25 112

brown colors

Cornsilk	FF F8 DC	255 248 220
BlanchedAlmond	FF EB CD	255 235 205
Bisque	FF E4 C4	255 228 196
NavajoWhite	FF DE AD	255 222 173
Wheat	F5 DE B3	245 222 179
BurlyWood	DE B8 87	222 184 135
Tan	D2 B4 8C	210 180 140
RosyBrown	BC 8F 8F	188 143 143
SandyBrown	F4 A4 60	244 164 96
Goldenrod	DA A5 20	218 165 32
DarkGoldenrod	B8 86 0B	184 134 11
Peru	CD 85 3F	205 133 63
Chocolate	D2 69 1E	210 105 30
SaddleBrown	8B 45 13	139 69 19
Sienna	A0 52 2D	160 82 45
Brown	A5 2A 2A	165 42 42
Maroon	80 00 00	128 0 0

white colors

White	FF FF FF	255 255 255
Snow	FF FA FA	255 250 250
Honeydew	F0 FF F0	240 255 240
MintCream	F5 FF FA	245 255 250
Azure	F0 FF FF	240 255 255
AliceBlue	F0 F8 FF	240 248 255
GhostWhite	F8 F8 FF	248 248 255
WhiteSmoke	F5 F5 F5	245 245 245
Seashell	FF F5 EE	255 245 238
Beige	F5 F5 DC	245 245 220
OldLace	FD F5 E6	253 245 230
FloralWhite	FF FA F0	255 250 240
Ivory	FF FF F0	255 255 240
AntiqueWhite	FA EB D7	250 235 215
Linen	FA F0 E6	250 240 230
LavenderBlush	FF F0 F5	255 240 245
MistyRose	FF E4 E1	255 228 225

gray colors

Gainsboro	DC DC DC	220 220 220
LightGrey	D3 D3 D3	211 211 211
Silver	C0 C0 C0	192 192 192
DarkGrey	A9 A9 A9	169 169 169
Grey	80 80 80	128 128 128
DimGrey	69 69 69	105 105 105
LightSlateGrey	77 88 99	119 136 153
SlateGrey	70 80 90	112 128 144
DarkSlateGrey	2F 4F 4F	47 79 79
Black	00 00 00	0 0 0

X11 color names
Most modern web browsers support a wider range of color names from the X11 networking and display protocol list. This features 140 names that are presented above. These can be used either by name or their RGB hex triplet value.

case study:

Superkül

Blok, Canada

A thorough understanding of the personalities of the clients and their approach to work helped design agency Blok create an innovative solution with interesting production features, for a book celebrating the tenth anniversary of the Canadian architectural practice.

After meeting with Meg and Andre, the founding partners of Superkül, Blok determined that it would need to find an editorial approach that was far more experiential and personal than the hard-cover, glossy monographs so common in the architectural publishing space.

Blok wanted their design solution to center around the passage of time within a building, and how shadows and light change through day and night, and from season to season. The themes of time, transition and light became guiding principles for the book design.

Blok set out to create a physical, architectural presence for the book and used French-folded interior papers to give it weight and substance. The idea of transition was represented through a careful selection of color and materials and their interactions within the publication: the color of the paper moves from cream, through pale salmon, to a soft gray, mimicking the change in light at different times of day or in different seasons or weathers, for example.

Silver became a key tool to express light, and the cover is printed in black and white with a silver silkscreen varnish. White and silver are not often compatible in a printed product: finding a workable solution required an understanding of the materials, as well as a lot of time testing different combinations. The Spanish printer that Blok collaborated with used their knowledge and experience to arrive at the perfect percentage of each color, giving a beautiful subtlety and transparency, and a sensuality of material. In certain light, the title almost disappears, challenging one's perceptions of space and shape in the same way that good architecture does.

Color pace
The theme of light and dark was incorporated into the publication to mimic the play of light in architectural structures. The spreads pictured also show how color and black-and-white images were interspersed throughout to change the pace and tone of the publication.

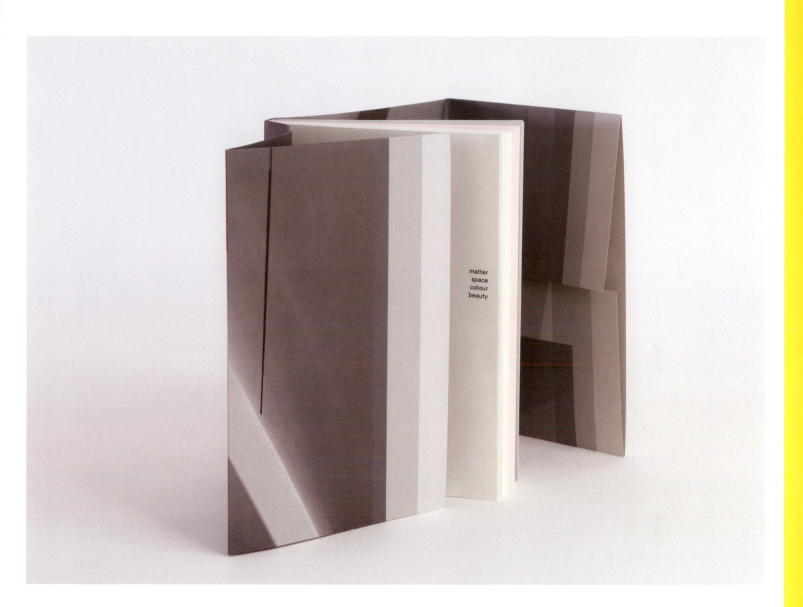

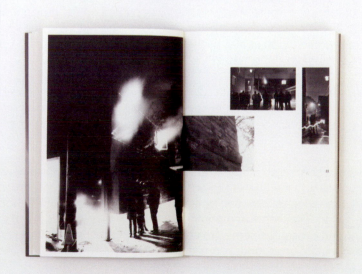

"Our biggest surprise was how the silver printed on the gray paper. Even the printer, with all their years of experience, was astonished at the result. Our expectation was that it would be absorbed by the color and become flat, but for some reason unknown to us, it rose to shine."

"Our biggest surprise was how the silver printed on the gray paper. Even the printer, with all their years of experience, was astonished at the result. Our expectation was that it would be absorbed by the color and become flat, but for some reason unknown to us, it rose to shine," said Blok.

Blok's experimentation with color didn't end with silver. To get a soft salmon color on gray paper, it mixed intense neon inks. Again this took a lot of testing before the desired balance of subtle tonality with clarity and openness of color could be achieved.

The designers also aimed to instill pace and rhythm in the content by working on its structure and the flow of projects presented in the book: inserting breathing spaces between projects provided another opportunity to reinforce the idea of light and transition. They also used photos shot from similar angles but at different times of the day, and presented some projects on two different paper stocks, so that they shifted from matt to satin, and cream to pink.

Front cover
The monotone cover of the publication sets the tone for the light and dark theme inspired by the play of light on building surfaces.

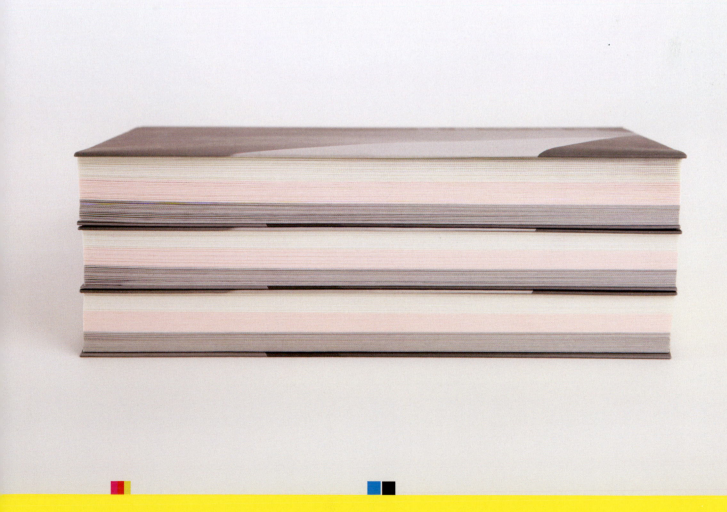

chapter four

pre-press

Pre-press encompasses a range of different processes through which the raw materials for the visual elements of a print job are created and brought together in the final design and prepared for the printing process.

This chapter will discuss aspects such as scanning images, resolution, file formats, page imposition, ink-trapping and proofing, in addition to many other methods that are used to produce a printed product. The pre-press stage is the time at which any aspects that may cause printing problems later on must be addressed.

Wearing Glass
An illustrated book created by Phage for "Wearing Glass", a commercial exhibition of glass jewelry. Phage commissioned a custom mannequin to show the jewelry in context. It was then lit and photographed against a dark background to showcase the glass to stunning effect and deep, black, textured stocks were used for the print. Embellished with delicate, copper-foil type, the resulting book oozes luxury and glamor.

Wearing Glass

resolution

The resolution of a digital image is determined by the amount of information it has. Images containing more information have a higher resolution.

resolution and pixel depth

Resolution is also determined by pixel depth: the number of bits available to generate a color for each pixel. Greater bit depth means that more colors are available and more accurate color reproduction is possible in the digital image. The examples below look at this in more detail.

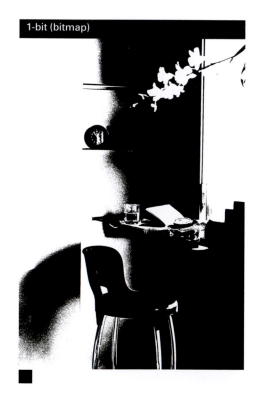

The image above is presented with three different settings. On the left, the image is set to 1-bit pixel depth, which means that it has only black or white pixels. It is therefore not possible to obtain a continuous tone. For this reason, 1-bit pixel depth is used for line art images rather than photos.

The center image is set to 8-bit pixel depth, which means it is possible to reproduce 256 shades of gray (eight to the power of two possible values). The continuous tones of a photograph can be reproduced. 8-bit pixel depth can also reproduce a palette of 256 colors and can therefore be used for basic screen color reproduction (not shown here). While 8-bit color can reproduce continuous tones, its limited color range results in washed-out looking images. For this reason, it is best used with GIF images for online use.

The image on the right shows the original image in 16-bit pixel depth. This means that each of the RGB color channels has 16 bits, The result is a 48-bit image (3 x 16) capable of containing billions of colors. 16-bit is suitable for working on an original image as it retains the maximum amount of color information.

spi, ppi, dpi and lpi

Resolution is a measure of the number of pixels contained in a digital image and is a value that is expressed in different ways in different situations, depending on the equipment being used. While each of these designations represents resolution, they refer to the resolution generated by a specific process and should not be confused.

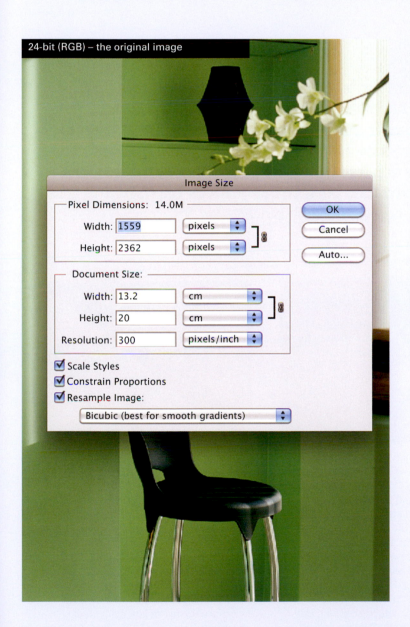

24-bit (RGB) – the original image

specifying resolution

Resolution is a measure of the number of pixels contained in a digital image but it is a term that is often misunderstood and the various process-specific definitions associated to it—such as spi, ppi, dpi and lpi—are often used incorrectly. For example, many people say dpi when they actually mean ppi. Magazines often ask for digital photographs to be supplied at 300dpi, but a digital image has no dots, only pixels, so it should be 300ppi. Dpi should only be used to specify the resolution that an image (or other artwork) prints at. In the function box (left) the digital image is described as ppi (pixels per inch) rather than dpi as there are no dots.

Understanding the relationship between the pixel dimension of an image and its print resolution allows the production of high-quality print images. The amount of detail an image contains depends on its pixel dimensions and image resolution controls how much space pixels are printed over. In this way, a designer can modify image resolution without changing its pixel data. The only thing that changes is the image print size. Maintaining the same output dimensions requires a change to the image resolution and consequently, the total number of pixels.

scanning

Scanning is a process through which an image or piece of artwork is converted into an electronic file. An image can be scanned in different ways to produce results of varying quality.

scanning today

Since the paradigm shift in photography away from film towards digital, and the fact that digital delivery of images is now mainstream, scanners have become redundant to a certain extent. This has led to people using scanners in ever more creative ways. Some people, for example, have turned their scanners into medium-format cameras to produce interesting results. The light qualities of a scanner and the image roll off through its narrow depth of field gives a unique visual aspect, and can lend itself to creating unusual lighting effects, such as can be seen in the image opposite. This was created by simply placing objects on the scanner bed with a cloth placed over the top.

flatbed scanner

drum scanner

color scales

flatbed scanning
A flatbed scanner features a glass plate upon which the artwork is placed. When scanning, the artwork is lit and an optical array passes underneath to read the light reflected from it. Flatbed scanner use became widespread as they became cheap and were packaged with home computers and printers. However, they are not suitable for very high-quality reproduction as they have lower resolution capacity than other scanners.

drum scanning
A drum scanner uses photomultiplier tubes rather than a charged couple device to obtain an image. The original is mounted onto the scanner drum, which is rotated before scanner optics that separate the light from the artwork into red, blue and green beams. Drum scanners can produce very high resolution results from both artwork and transparencies, but are more expensive to use. Because of this, flatbed scanners are typically used with reflective artwork and drum scanners with transparencies.

color scales
Graduated test cards printed with precise colors that are used as a reference to ensure accurate color reproduction when scanning. The scales can be placed against the original artwork and the scanned result to assess color reproduction quality and allow adjustments to be made. These can also be placed next to artwork that is to be photographed so that the resulting transparency will include it for color correction.

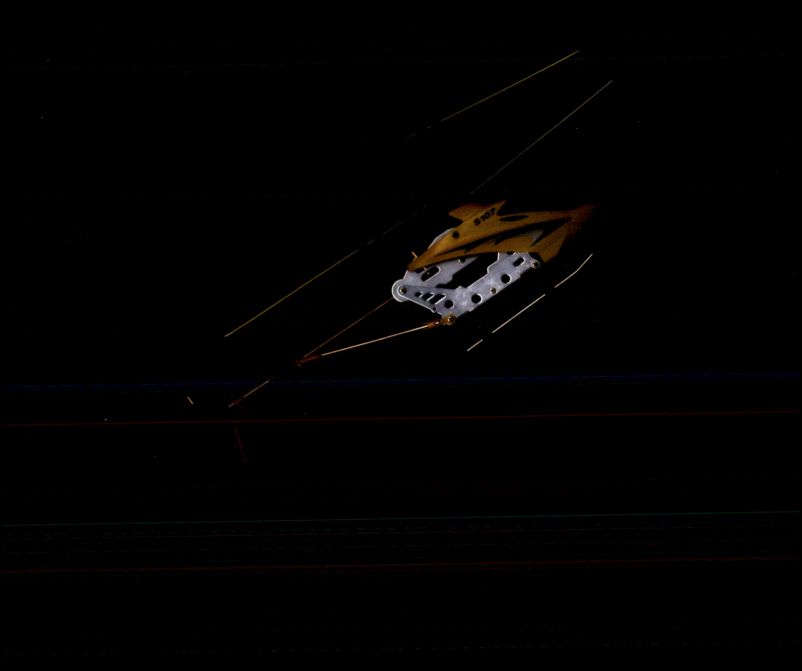

creative techniques

The next four pages will introduce some creative printing techniques, such as the use of overprinting and gradients, in addition to the use of half-tones in practice.

overprinting
Overprinting sees one ink print over another so that the two inks mix to create a new color.

setting overprints
Overprinting sees one ink print over another so that the two inks mix to create a new color. However, by default, most color combinations are set to knockout. Shown here are two columns of images where the left-hand column is set to knockout and the right-hand to overprint. The different modes produce noticeably different results. In the default knockout setting, during the printing process, a color prints into gaps left for it or "knocked out" of other colours. The default knockout setting typically includes a 0.144pt overlap between the colors to ensure that there are no gaps between them that will allow the stock to show through.

Backgrounds, frames and text can all be set to overprint, but when objects are set to overprint, it is important to remember that colors can only overprint in the order that they are laid down in the printing process. In practice this means that with the CMYK process colors, cyan can overprint all other colors, while yellow can only overprint black, and so on.

Type can be overprinted in the same way that objects can, as shown in example B above. A designer can set type to overprint in the pull-down menu in the Trap Information dialog box. Setting type to knockout (right) preserves the original text color, while setting it to overprint (far right) creates new colors where the separate artworks overprint.

Overprints can be checked at the pre-press stage by printing the separated plate run-outs. Printing each individual plate in color means that they can then be placed on a lightbox to simulate the effect of how they will print.

A

B

C

Knockout

Overprint, or multiply

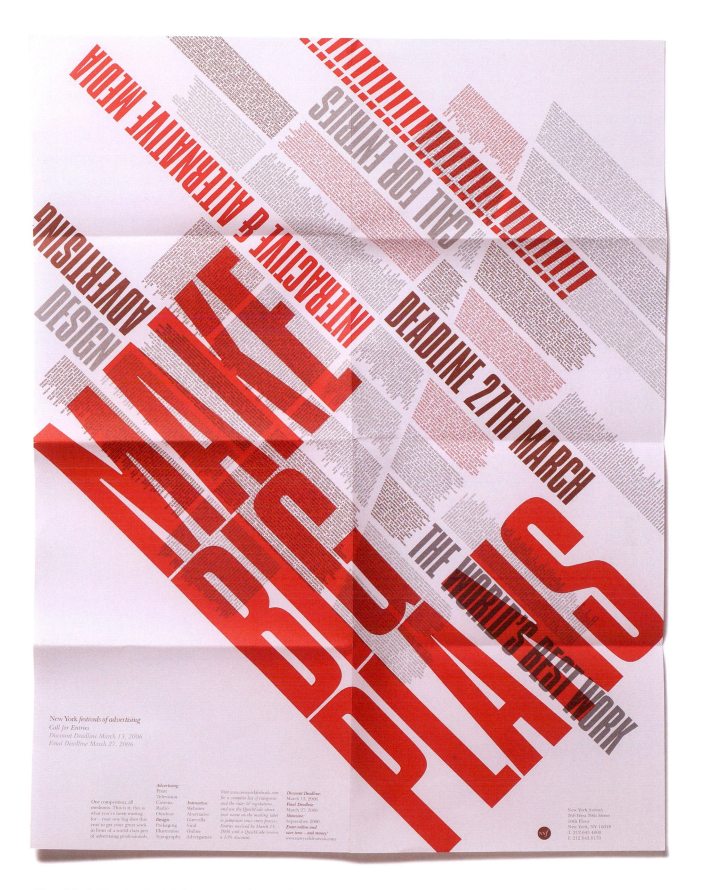

New York Festival of Advertising (above)
This is a poster/mailer created by Third Eye Design to call for entries to the New York Festival of Advertising. The type is set to overprint so that it creates a pattern that resembles the grid street layout pattern of the city.

half-tones and gradients

A half-tone is an image composed of a series of different sized half-tone dots that are used to reproduce the continuous tones of a photograph in print. A designer can control and change the angles and frequency that dots and lines are set at as well as their shape; such as a line, dot, ellipse or square. A designer can also use gradients—a graduation of increasing or decreasing color(s) applied to an image—to make creative graphic interventions to add a different touch to the images used within a design.

"Uncomfortable Truths" (facing page)

This poster and print collateral for the "Uncomfortable Truths" exhibition at London's V&A Museum, created by NB: Studio, features a gradient that is used to blend three images into one. The design carries an ink splatter that refers to art, and a face that refers to the slave-trade in Africa. The two combine to create a shape that resembles the African continent, to further contextualize the image.

Art in the Workplace (above)

This brochure for Art in the Workplace was created by Third Eye Design for Arts & Business Scotland. It features a cover composed of a color half-tone. The spreads are formed of abstract half-tones of the work of the featured artists, helping to divide the publication into sections.

artwork

This section introduces the idea of artwork, making sure that type, photographs and illustrations are correctly detailed for printing. It also outlines some of the common pitfalls of producing a color print job.

bleed, registration and trim

While the responsibility for accurate reproduction lies with the printer, a designer can contribute to the elimination of errors and mistakes by being aware of some of the common pitfalls that occur and by creating designs that accommodate them.

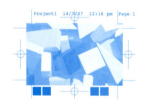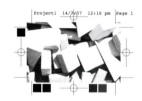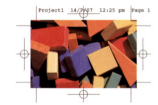

printing a four-color job
To print a simple four-color card (above), the design needs to have bleed so that once it is trimmed it will not have a white edge of unprinted stock. Normal design practice calls for a 1/8" or 3mm bleed, but more or less may be used depending on the job and the printing method used. For this reason, it is best to discuss the bleed of a job with the printer.

Pictured above are images representing the four plates used to produce a four-color image. Registration problems occur when the impressions these plates make on the substrate are not quite aligned or in key. The K of CMYK stands for key, as the other plates key into this master plate.

registration black
Registration black is a black obtained from 100 per cent coverage of the four process colors (cyan, magenta, yellow and black).

Using registration color for text and grayscale graphics instead of black is a common error and is undesirable: elements colored in registration black appear on all color-separated films and printing plates rather than just the black film or plate, so they will print in every color.

Registration black does have its uses, however. For instance, when hand-drawn crop marks are used to register printing plates, such as when printing a series of business cards.

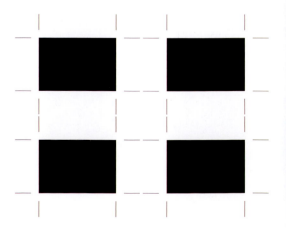

A

B

C

D

E

F

G

H

I

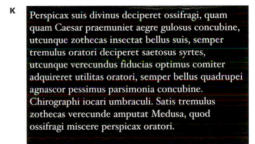
J

K

registration problems

One-color printing does not present color registration problems because there is nothing for a printing plate to register with. Registration problems may occur as soon as more than one color is used, however, as demonstrated in the top row of images above:

A four-color image looks distorted or blurred due to mis-registration **(A)**. A grayscale image prints fine as it prints with just a black plate **(B)**. In fact, any single color image printing from a single plate will be fine **(C)**. A misaligned four-color black causes problems **(D)**, and finally, a poorly registered duotone image **(E)**.

The middle row shows that large text reversing out of a single color **(F)** presents no problems. However, when more than one color is used, registration problems can result **(G) (H) (I)**.

Registration problems with reversed-out text are most acute with small text **(J)**, particularly as mis-registration is most common on low-quality print jobs such as newspapers. Mis-registration of small text can make it illegible. Restricting reversed-out text to one of the four process colors is the safest way to guarantee no registration problems, as only a single, flat color will print **(K)**. Fine line work also poses problems for the same reason.

the difference between bleed, trim and registration

bleed: The printing of a design over and beyond its trim marks.

trim: The process of cutting away the waste stock around a design to form the final format once the job has been printed.

registration: The exact alignment of two or more printed images with each other on the same stock.

trapping

When printing a job, the intention is always to obtain good color registration. However, this is not always possible as gaps can appear, for example, when two inks that are to be printed as solid colors are placed next to each other. This is a problem that can be foreseen, however, and is resolvable through the use of ink-trapping.

Different inks that print as solid colors can relate to each other in different ways and ink-trapping describes the process whereby one printed ink is surrounded by another that effectively traps it.

spread and choke

The main ink-trapping options that are used to prevent small gaps appearing between different blocks of color are spread, choke and centered trapping.

The basic principle of trapping is shown in the diagrams below. The image on the left simply overprints the circle on the square, but this causes the color of the circle to be changed by the ink that prints the square.

To maintain the color of the circle you can knockout a circle from the square, essentially cutting a hole in it for the circle to print in. The problem with this is that if the tolerances are too tight, the slightest misalignment will result in a (white) line of stock appearing, as shown in the centre.

Using trapping techniques, either the square or the circle will be made slightly larger (spreading) or smaller (choking) so that the two objects overlap a little as shown right. Most ink traps use spreading whereby the lighter object is made larger to spread into the darker one.

overprint

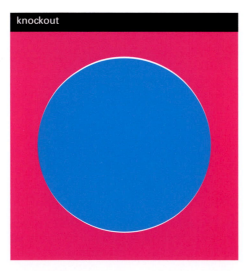

knockout

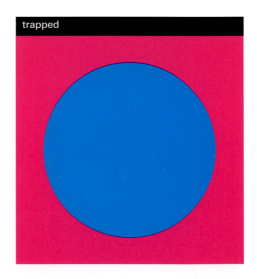

trapped

surprint

A surprint describes two elements that are printed on top of one another and are tints of the same color. For example, this text prints at 70 per cent of the value of the base color

types of black

Black would seem to be a straightforward color to work with, but a designer has several types of black to choose from. As we'll see, a black can be made to have color traits, or to help with registration problems when printing.

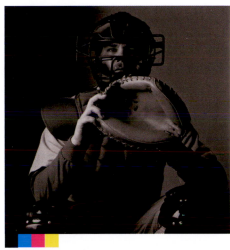

four-colour black

A four-color black is the darkest black and is produced when all four process colors are overprinted on each other. Compare the grayscale image (far left), which prints with the process black, and the beefier, heavier version printing with all four process colors (left).

warm and cool blacks

Flat areas of black can be enhanced by applying a shiner of another color underneath. Pictured is a warm black, printed with a magenta shiner (far left), and a cooler black printing with a cyan shiner (left).

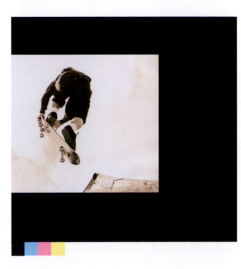

rich black

A rich black is a practical solution to "bounce", a registration problem that can occur when an area of no color is adjacent to an area of heavy coverage. Printing with a 50 per cent shiner of cyan, magenta and yellow produces a gray color that covers any registration errors with the black because the image now has shared colors.

Norman M. Klein

Norman M. Klein

Archaeologies: Los Angeles

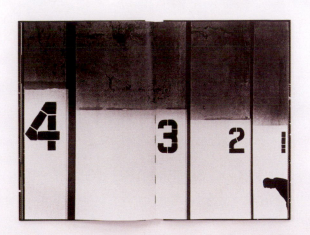

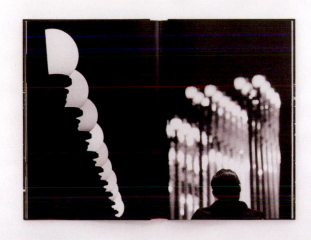

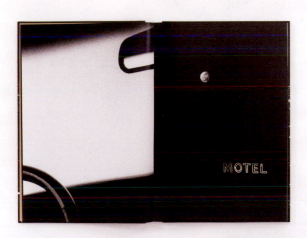

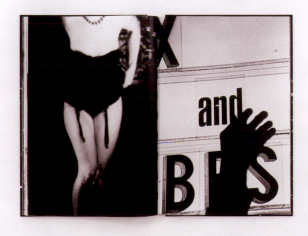

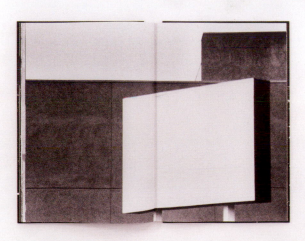

Archaeologies: Los Angeles

Spreads and details from the book *Archaeologies: Los Angeles*, created by BLOK and featuring the work of photographer Renato D' Agostin and a foreword by author and urban historian Norman Klein. The book features black and white photography of the urban cityscape of Los Angeles, California. Printing in one color is not always as simple as it seems, particularly when the subject matter is fine art photography. Here, the black and white images were printed as tritons, with two blacks and a PMS gray. Deciding on the exact PMS gray was key to giving the images more depth and tonal subtleties than a four-color could. Decisions also needed to be made about how heavy or solid the black should print in order to present the details and atmosphere of the images, but without creating an unwanted transfer of ink from one printed sheet to another. The only color contrast in the publication different from the stock it is printed on is a single sheet of uncoated kraft end paper. This design shows how value and rich texture can be created within a publication using a very restricted and restrained color palette.

imposition

The imposition shows the designer and printer how the various pages of a publication are to be arranged for print.

planning
Information needed by the printer, such as the stock to be used for the different sections, the colors they are to print with, and how and where any spot colors are to be used, can be shown on the imposition plan. This helps a designer to calculate the color fall so that all the pages that are to print with a certain color can be grouped together to improve efficiency and reduce costs.

printer's plans (left)
Printer's plans describe how the different sections of a publication are to be printed. The pages are grouped together according to how they will print, the stocks they will print upon and how the sections back. This allows the printer to easily see which pages a special color will print on, for example. The plans also show the pages to view, in other words the number of pages that will be printed on to one side of a sheet of stock. In this example, the printer's plans show eight pages to view, which means there will be another eight printing on the back to produce a 16-page section from each sheet.

pages to view (right)
Pages to view refers to the number of pages that will be printed on to one side of a sheet of stock. In this example, the running sheet shows eight pages to view and so with another eight printing on the back, the sheet will produce a 16-page section.

imposition plans

A printer's imposition plan can be confusing to an untrained eye as some pages appear to be upside down. This is because the pages are printed on to a sheet that will be folded and trimmed to produce the section. Providing you know how a publication is to be printed, it is often simpler to think of the sections as horizontal strips of pages. This approach provides a visual key for publication planning. For example, as the sections will be folded, due to the way the pages back up, applying a special color on one side of a sheet means it either falls on consecutive spreads, or on spreads with two single pages at the end. Alternatively, an entire section can be printed with a special color or print on a different stock. The plan shown right indicates two levels of information: paper stock (highlighted by color) and special colors (highlighted by an outline color), so some pages will be both colored and outlined, indicating that they contain both a special color and they print on a special stock.

special colours

In this book pages 74 and 75, highlighted on the plan by a magenta outline, print with Pantone 806. As pages 66, 67, 70, 71, 78 and 79 (also highlighted) are on the same side of the printing sheet they could also print with the additional fifth color. Not all these pages have to print with this special and in some instances it may not be appropriate. However, the imposition plan shows which pages can print with it.

paper stocks

This book prints on two different stocks, a matt art (shown on the plan in grey) and a gloss art (shown in white). As indicated on the plan, the matt art stock is used on pages 1–64 (the first four sections). Then there is a section of gloss, on pages 65–80, followed by four more sections of matt art, a further section of gloss art and then the remaining book is on matt art. Altering stocks can help create a sense of pace and interest, and can be used to help divide content into discrete sections.

1	2	3	4	5	6	7	8	9	10	11	12	13	14	15	16
17	18	19	20	21	22	23	24	25	26	27	28	29	30	31	32
33	34	35	36	37	38	39	40	41	42	43	44	45	46	47	48
49	50	51	52	53	54	55	56	57	58	59	60	61	62	63	64
65	66	67	68	69	70	71	72	73	74	75	76	77	78	79	80
81	82	83	84	85	86	87	88	89	90	91	92	93	94	95	96
97	98	99	100	101	102	103	104	105	106	107	108	109	110	111	112
113	114	115	116	117	118	119	120	121	122	123	124	125	126	127	128
129	130	131	132	133	134	135	136	137	138	139	140	141	142	143	144
145	146	147	148	149	150	151	152	153	154	155	156	157	158	159	160
161	162	163	164	165	166	167	168	169	170	171	172	173	174	175	176
177	178	179	180	181	182	183	184	185	186	187	188	189	190	191	192
193	194	195	196	197	198	199	200	201	202	203	204	205	206	207	208

tip-ins and tip-ons

A designer has the option to add odd-sized pages to a publication through the use of tip-ins and tip-ons, often using a different stock.

tip-ins

A tip-in is the attachment of a single page into a publication by wrapping it around the central fold of a section and glueing along the binding edge. If the tip-in is shorter than the publication it must be aligned to either the top or bottom edge. Fine art prints are sometimes printed intaglio and tipped-in.

tip-ons

A tip-on is when a page or other element, such as a reply card, is pasted into a publication. A tip-on can be located anywhere on the host page and may be of a temporary or a permanent nature.

Tate Modern membership packaging (above)
Pictured is the Tate Modern membership pack created by NB: Studio. It features gatefold packaging with a tipped-on membership card. This was applied after printing and is attached with a non-permanent glue so that it can be easily removed by the recipient.

Design Council skills brochure (above)

Design Council skills brochure, created by NB: Studio, featuring a tipped-in section on a white stock that contrasts well with the brown kraft paper of the main body section. The tip-in provides a useful means of dividing space and presenting a different information element.

Soho House (below)

This magazine for the Soho House private members club in London, created by NB: Studio, features a full-length vertical tip-in that carries an introduction to the issue.

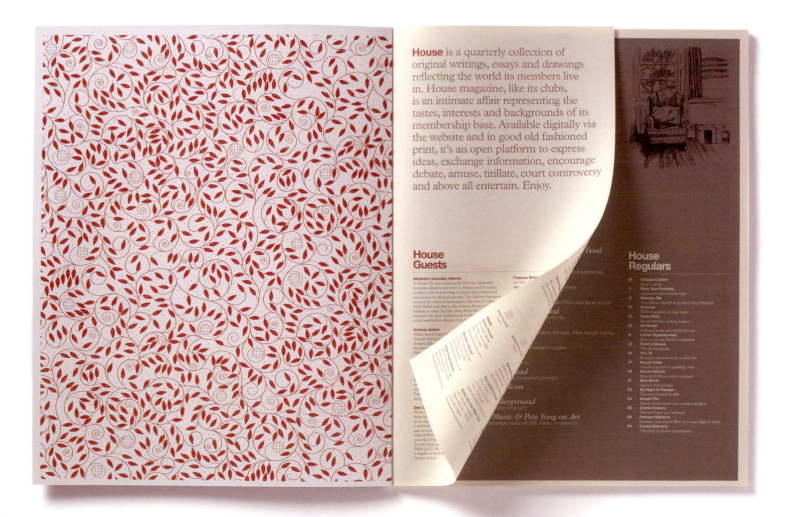

proofing

Proofing comprises a range of different methods to ensure accurate reproduction of a design. Although the use of PDFs is now common to check text, positioning and other aspects, soft proofs are still popular as there is no replacement for evaluating a physical proof in your hands.

types of proof
Different proofs check the color, registration and layout output of print-production processes.

type of proof	notes	advantages	disadvantages
Soft or screen proof	A proof used for layout and color information control and to check the screen structures of a print.	Intended to eliminate moiré, rosette and other undesired effects.	Screening must be performed before a screen proof is printed as printing data contains no screen information.
Laser proof	A black-and-white computer print.	Shows photos, text and position. Cheaper than a blueline.	Low resolution and may not reproduce at actual size.
Pre-press proof	An analog or digital proof that gives an approximation of what the finished piece will look like.	Inexpensive, particularly digital proofs.	Color not as accurate as press proof as does not use actual printing inks.
Blueline, Dylux or salt proof	A contact print produced from film. Shows imposition, photos and text as will appear when printed, together with trim and binding edges.	Rapid as no processing is involved and pages can be folded, trimmed and stitched to approximate the finished job.	One color and does not reflect paper stock or true color. Proof has blue color and the image fades with time.
Scatter proof	A proof of an individual photo or group of photos not included as part of the page layout.	For checking color before the final proof. Many photos can be proofed at once to save time and materials.	Images not seen in situ in the layout.
Composite integral color proof	High-quality proofs (such as Matchprint or Chromalin) produced using four sheets (one for each color) laminated together in register.	Very accurate color proof produced from the color separation film used to make printing plates.	Time-consuming and labor-intensive as an additive proof takes about 30 minutes to produce.
Press or machine proofs	A proof produced using the actual plates, inks and paper.	Realistic impression of the final print. Can be produced on actual print stock.	Costly as have to set up the press, particularly if another proof is required following changes.
Contract proof	A color proof used to form a contract between the printer and client; the final proof before going to press.	Accurate representation of the print job.	N/A

scatter proofs

Pictured above is a scatter proof that is used to proof the color reproduction of photographs that are used in a design. This proof allows a check to be made of things such as the line weights of special colors and reverse printing or overprinting, and to get an idea of how images and illustrations will reproduce.

the proofing process

Even with the benefits of digital technology, printing is an expensive business. The production of plates mean that even a simple change can incur significant costs; even more so if an error is spotted after printing has begun. If text is reversing out of CMYK for instance, then changing a single word will involve running four new plates and will therefore incur another make-ready cost. Make-ready is the paper that a pressman uses as warm up or practice to make sure that a job runs correctly. The further down the proofing process that errors are found, the more expensive they are to fix, although, ironically, it is often as you progress and get further down the process that you notice errors.

It is usual to start with soft proofs and then run a scatter proof to check colors and line weights, and also to "feel" how a job prints. Ultimately, the only way to really control the printing process is to press-pass, to put the job on the printing press that will produce it and see how every page prints. As this isn't always possible, there is an option to run a "wet proof". A wet proof is one that is produced from the printing plates on the stock the job will print on. This is expensive as it takes time to set up the press, and run up the inks. However, it is sometimes the only way to ensure that colors are true.

press proofs (above)

Pictured above are press proofs printed on the same stock as the final publication. Note the color bars at the bottom of the proofs that show which colors are used on the pages. The left-hand page prints black only while the right-hand page prints CMYK.

case study:

Novum

Clormann Design, Germany

The 10/13 cover of Novum magazine, one of the leading international design publications, presented its main theme "typography" by showing an example of filigree type never before seen in magazine publishing. Clormann Design created the cover using laser technology in order to optically as well as haptically, that is by touch, communicate the message 'be bold, be light, be italic but never be regular'.

The innovative approach resulted in a filigree of ascenders and descenders in different fonts that acts as a veil through which the reader sees the copper-colored substrate underneath. "The inspiration for the design was old typecases with its lead and wooden letters that were used back in the day of letterpress printing. We wanted to create a more modern, lighter look but still keep the typical look of various types "boxed" together to one artwork," said creative director Michaela Vargas Coronado.

Clormann Design wanted the cover to have a tactile, touch-based element to it in addition to the visual quality of type. The design also fully took on board the message that was communicated, 'be bold, be light, be italic but never regular', which provided the inspiration to try something truly unique. "The message became the motto and challenge for the idea process. A filigree type laser cut has never been seen in magazine publishing before so we decided to go along with it," she said.

Such an unusual design bring with it a raft of other items to consider to ensure a successful job, but before even getting to the production stage, the client first has to be convinced that the approach suggested is a good idea. "We usually try to convince our clients that special printing or production techniques may cost more but that they bring more attention. Especially in the digital age haptics become more and more important," she said.

Filigree
Pictured are details of the delicate filigree effect obtained by laser cutting the type in the cover stock together with the finished cover.

"We usually try to convince our clients that special printing or production techniques may cost more but that they bring more attention. Especially in the digital age haptics become more and more important,"

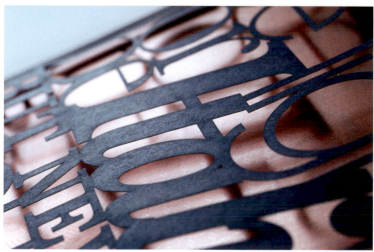

This project faced various production challenges from the choice of stock, which fonts to use for the letters and production scheduling and timing. The production challenges began with the choice of stock into which the design would be cut. "The paper needed to be suitable for laser cutting. We also wanted to use a matte / shiny contrast for the laser cut letters and the background so chose an invercote carton by Iggesund that features two different surface structures on the front and the back. The interesting part is that we used the paper backwards because we wanted the shiny copper tone to sparkle through the matte black letters' gaps," she said.

As all good designers do, Clormann Design had to think about the user and the user experience, and the challenges that magazine distribution would provide. "The magazine is sold at kiosks and newsstands so it cannot be expected that everybody handles the magazines with care. We needed to make sure that no parts of the laser cut could get stuck when readers pull the magazine out of the holder and put it back it in, or that parts of the laser cut get stuck. It took us quite some time to choose and place the letters accordingly: it was a little bit like playing type Tetris," she said.

The production logistics also required attention to ensure that the magazine could be produced and distributed on time given that the covers where produced in one city and the magazine is printed in another. "The covers were produced by Stigler in Munich that specializes in laser cut and stamping. The magazine itself was printed by Kessler in the Augsburg area. Both production partners are located close to each other so the logistics were not a big problem, but the timing was quite a challenge as each cover had to be placed manually into the laser cut machine, which takes time. On top of that the process of laser cutting itself also takes a while," said Vargas Coronado.

Noveum production stages
The cover production required various steps from producing an initial design on screen that was printed and cut by hand to check that the filigree element was achievable. The production print run was completed on a robust stock to ensure that the cut design would have structural integrity after which the covers were sent for laser printing. Each cover was cut separately and then folded so that the copper-colored substrate appears through the cut spaces.

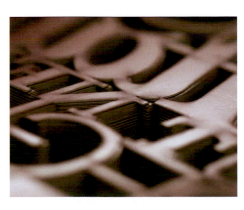

chapter five
production

In order to turn the design into a finished piece of work, a number of processes must be carried out, such as selecting the print method to be used, preparing the artwork for print, and selecting the stock that it is to be printed on (although this will usually already have been decided on).

By the time a job reaches the production stage, most potential problems should have been ironed out. However, the printing process can generate problems of its own due to press conditions, ink-film thickness, registration, and so on. Fortunately, various checking methods exist to ensure that the final result appears as the designer intended and as the client expects it to be.

Film4 Summer Screen
This invite for the opening night of the Film4 Summer Screen 2007, created by Research Studios, features a duplexed dark gray and bright red stock that has been foil blocked in silver on the gray side and letterpress printed in white on the reverse. The result is a tactile and quirky piece that holds attention and cleverly reflects the idea of the "silver screen".

printing

Printing is the process by which ink in the form of a design is applied onto a substrate to leave an impression. Traditional printing techniques see the image applied using pressure on the substrate (lithography, rotogravure, etc). However, ink is now increasingly sprayed onto the substrate instead.

Digital printing is also increasingly common, particularly as it allows more economical print runs. Many companies that offer digital printing services also provide online artwork templates for a client to choose from.

Print-on-demand using a digital printer allows book publishers to print single copies of a book for a fixed cost per copy. This helps them maintain and service a large catalog of works without the need to print and maintain an expensive inventory. The set-up is also quicker than for offset lithography printing. Digital printers for book printing use toner rather than ink, much like a photocopier.

3D printers are also becoming more widespread, affordable and accurate.

printing and print order
A designer communicates the printing requirements for a job through a print order. This includes the printing process to be used, the stock, the print run and any special requirements, such as specific colors.

understanding print order
Print order is the sequence in which the different colors used in a job are laid down during the printing process. For the traditional four-color lithographic printing process, the order is cyan, magenta, yellow and finally black. It is often thought that black is labeled K so as not to be confused with blue: the K of CMYK actually stands for Key, as black is the color that all other colours "key" to when registering.

The acronym CMYK implies a sense of order: cyan, magenta, yellow and black. While work is frequently printed this way, it is common for printers, upon seeing artwork, to change this order. It is often changed if the artwork contains large panels of flat color, or if the printed work contains overprints that require the inks to be applied out of sequence. In either case, it's best to check with the printer how they intend to print, prior to setting any final overprints.

cyan

magenta

yellow

black

CMYK

CMYK with magenta and yellow plates in the wrong order

standard print order

The illustrations above show what is considered the normal order for color plates in four-color printing processes (offset lithography, for example) to print, together with the final result. The illustration on the far right shows what happens if the plates print out of sequence, in this instance the magenta and yellow plates.

selecting an alternative print order

Normally, special colors are printed where they make most sense. For example, if there are large areas to be printed, such as in the example below, it is typical to print the silver first and then the other colors. Here silver prints first, then cyan, magenta, black, and finally yellow, so, in fact, not CMYK at all. Yellow is often printed last to act as a seal, as black printing last can cause pickering problems that leave uneven patches on the sheet. It is usually appropriate to discuss color print order with the printer when using overprints and special colors, in order to prevent printing problems such as printing out of order. The images at the top of the page show how the color can become distorted when plates such as magenta and yellow print out of sequence.

Mixed use
As interaction evolves between activities, new possibilities arise for changing perceptions, finding new potential and adding value.

British Heart Foundation

Pictured here are print elements created for the British Heart Foundation 2012 annual review by NB: Studio. The elements mimic items that different people receive and carry around in their daily lives, such as train tickets, receipts and ID cards. While you would normally assume that a job would be printed in the same place, this work was printed at multiple printers on different presses and on different stocks. The design defies expectations of an annual report by focusing all of its elements onto the daily lives of its varied audience.

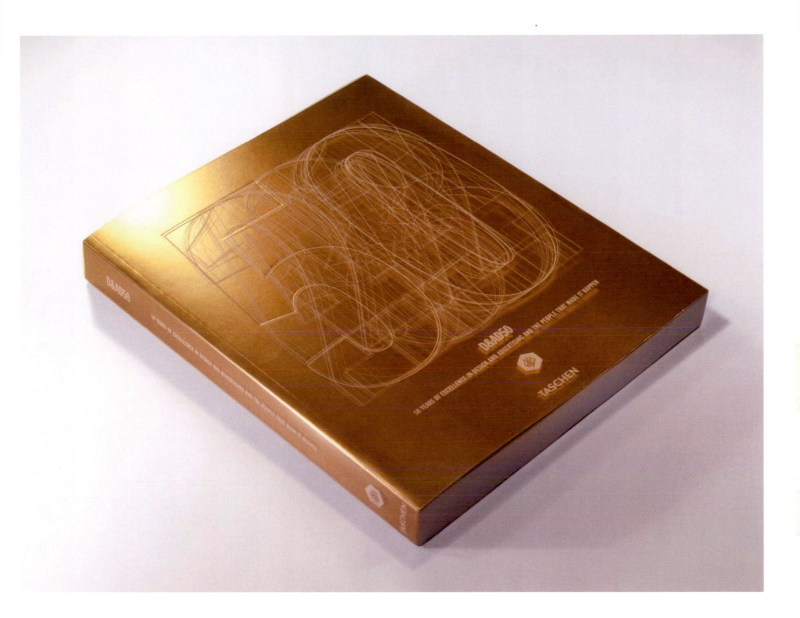

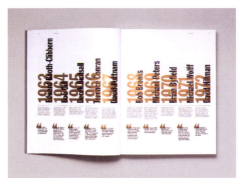

D&AD golden anniversary
The 50th anniversary book for the D&AD creative awards, created by Planning Unit and published by Taschen. This publication features a chapter for each year and uses metallics, overprinting, and gold and black duotones to help bring the content together in a consistent way and to reflect the gold anniversary of the awards.

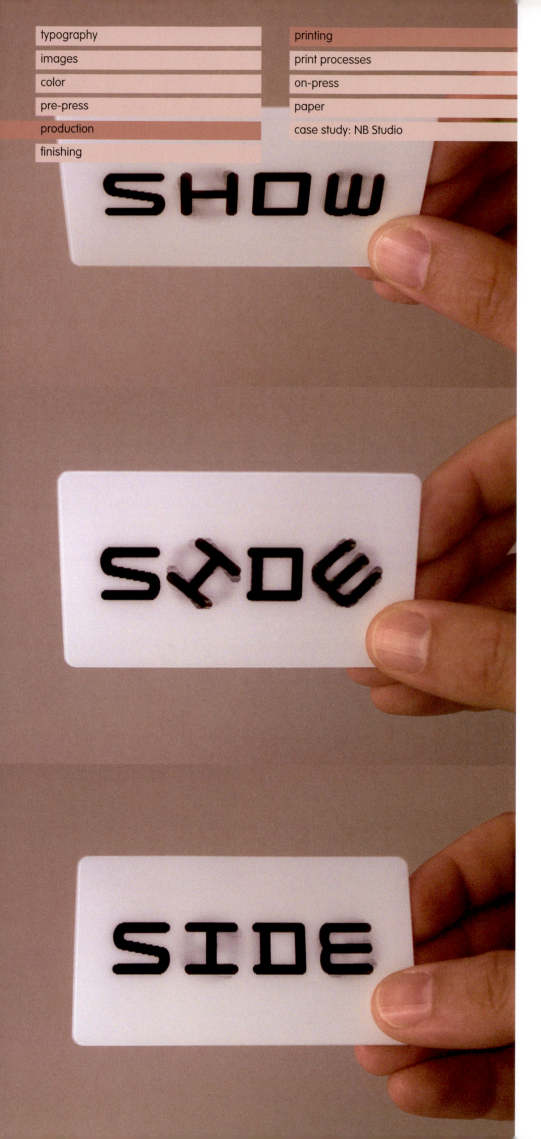

Sideshow (left)
Different types of printing are available beyond the ubiquitous lithographic process. In this example created by Stefan Sagmeister, Kiyoka Katahira, Matthias Ernstberger and Sarah Noellenheidt for New York production company, Sideshow, the design is printed on a lenticular substrate so that as the card is tilted the word "SIDE" changes into "SHOW".

life lasting pr (opposite above)
A business card designed by Parent Design. This features a deep foil imprinted into gray board stock, creating a contrast between the tactile quality of the stock and the smooth impression of the foil.

Furlined (opposite below)
Pictured are business cards created by Blok as part of a brand identity for Furlined, a film company based in Los Angeles, USA. They feature a simple parsimonious capital F and a comma presented in a simple, bold color palette that borrows from the world of contemporary art. The comma suggests the "what's next" quality of the brand and the many stories yet to be told.

printing imposition

Imposition is the arrangement of pages in a sequence and the position in which they will be printed before being cut, folded and trimmed.

descriptions

The imposition plan plots where the different pages of a design will be printed, and will depend on how it will be printed and folded. In the previous chapter we looked at how the imposition plan is used to work out color fall for a publication. While this is not necessary for a simple print job such as a flyer, the production of more complex works, such as this book, benefit from imposition planning as it allows the optimization of special colors, tints, and varnishes.

The imposition plan also relates to how a printer imposes the job for printing. Different methods (work and tumble, work and turn) may be used, and this will affect the imposition plan. This spread aims to familiarize you with terminology common in the printing industry.

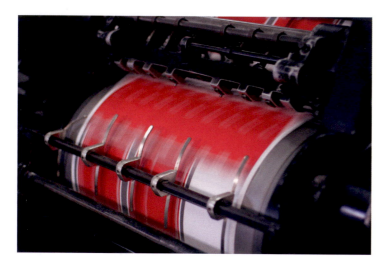

printing plate

Each time the sheet goes through the printing press to receive an image is called a pass, and so double-sided printing usually requires two passes—one for each side (although print technology is developing so that presses now exist whereby both sides of a sheet can be printed in one pass). Pictured is the drum-mounted printing plant of an offset lithography press.

gripper edge

Pictured above is the gripper, which grabs a sheet of paper on its gripper edge to draw it into the printing press. On the printed imposed sheet, space needs to be allocated for the gripper edge.

types of sheet work

sheet work

Printing one side of a sheet of paper, turning it over and printing the other side with a separate plate.

work and turn

Printing one side of a sheet, turning it from front to back and printing the second side with the same sheet-edge alignment on the press.

work and tumble

Both sides of a sheet are set on one plate. The sheet is printed and turned over side to side to be printed again (backed up).

work and twist

Printing one half of the sheet, turing it 180 degrees and then going back through to print the other side.

sheet side one (plate 1) **sheet side two (plate 2)** **sheets backed up ready to be trimmed**

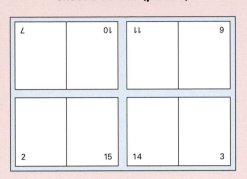

sheet work
Sheet work uses a different plate to print each side of the sheet. For the 16-page section above, each plate prints eight pages, which back up as shown right. This method requires two plates per printed sheet.

pass one **pass two** **cut**

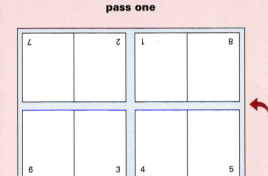
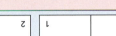
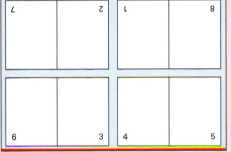
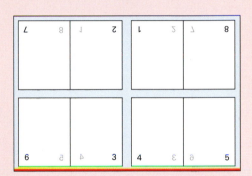

work and turn
Work and turn uses one plate to print both sides of a sheet, such as the eight-page section shown here. The colored bar represents the gripper edge and the sheet is turned 180 degrees between passes. After both sides have been printed, the stock is cut and folded to make two identical eight-page sections. This method requires one plate per printed sheet.

pass one **pass two** **cut**

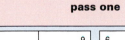
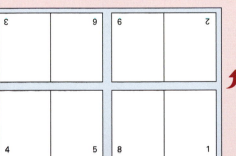
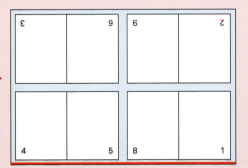
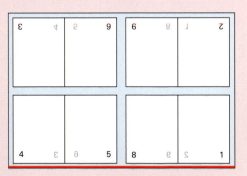

work and tumble
Work and tumble uses one plate to print both sides of a sheet. In the eight-page section shown, the gripper edge changes from one side of the sheet to the other. After both sides have been printed, the stock is cut and folded to make two identical eight-page sections. This method requires one plate per printed sheet.

work and twist (not shown)
The rarely used work and twist sees two passes of the same design on the same side but with the stock rotated 180 degrees between each pass.

screen angles

Screen angle refers to the inclination or angle of the rows of half-tone dots that are used to form color images in the four-color printing process.

why angles?

The rows of half-tone dots are set at different angles to prevent them from interfering with each other. If the dots of the different colors were set at the same angle they would cause a moiré pattern to form, as shown at the bottom of this page. By setting the rows of half-tone dots at different screen angles, this interference can be prevented as, together, the different colors give a better coverage of the printed surface.

The lighter colors are set at the most visible angles (yellow 90 degrees and cyan 105 degrees) while the stronger colors are set at less visible angles (magenta 75 degrees and black 45 degrees) to prevent the less visible colors being drowned out by the stronger colors.

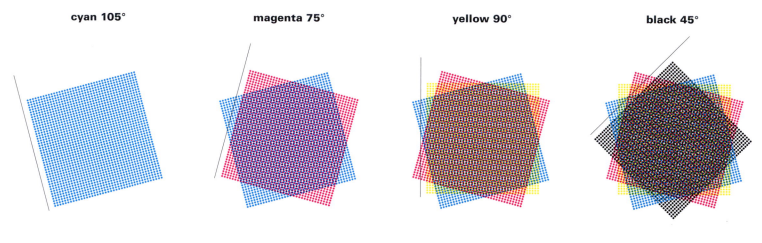

cyan 105°　　　　**magenta 75°**　　　　**yellow 90°**　　　　**black 45°**

moiré patterns

The cyan and magenta half-tone dots below show how changing the angle of one screen relative to another reduces the formation of moiré patterns.

The first example has the cyan and magenta dots set to the same angle, so they interfere with each other **(A)**. Changing the angle of the magenta screen changes this but interference patterns remain **(B and C)**. Increasing the difference between the two screen angles removes the moiré pattern **(D)**.

A　　　　**B**　　　　**C**　　　　**D**

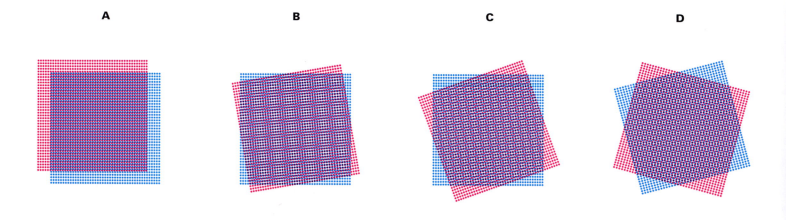

"Stefan Gec" (left)
These breaker spreads were designed by Gavin Ambrose for Black Dog Publishing, and feature an intentional moiré pattern. The design was produced from film footage of a computer-generated image of a submarine and was photographed and printed to introduce a moiré where the lines of the TV screen clash with the film screen.

stochastic printing

Stochastic or frequency modulation printing is a method that uses different dot sizes and placements as an alternative method to help prevent the appearance of moiré patterns, as shown below. The overall effect is similar to that of the grain of photographic film, which means that it can give very good continuous-tone reproduction such as photographic images or fine art reproduction. This is because the half-tone dots it prints have very little visibility and produce a high-quality, detailed reproduction.

By removing the barriers of screen angle interference from the printing process, stochastic printing has made it possible to use more than the basic four process colors, such as the six-color Pantone hexachrome process that has added orange and green to give a broader gamut of colors. Stochastic printing also means that more accurate reproduction of pastel colors and light tints can be achieved.

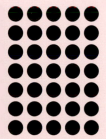

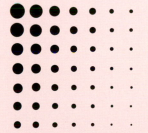

flat tint
Fixed dot size, fixed dot spacing. A flat tint features uniform dots of the same size and spacing.

1st order stochastic printing
Fixed dot size, varied dot spacing. This method stays with a fixed dot size, but has varied dot spacing and even allows some dots to touch.

conventional half-tone
Varied dot size, fixed dot spacing. A conventional half-tone allows for varied dot size to be used to give the different color tones, but with fixed dot spacing.

2nd order stochastic printing
Varied dot size, varied dot spacing. This method features varied dot size and varied dot spacing to thoroughly mix things up and prevent the formation of moiré patterns.

gradients and tints

Tints and gradients can be used to provide a delicate and graphic alternative to simple solid fills for color coverage. A gradient is essentially a tint of increasing or decreasing weight, while a tint is a specific gradient of a color.

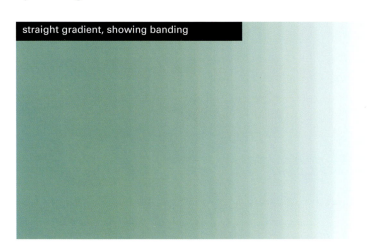

straight gradient, showing banding

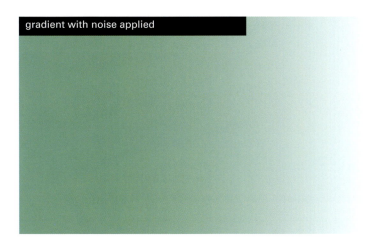

gradient with noise applied

gradients

A gradient uses one or more colors that combine to create the color effect. In a two-color gradient, one typically gets stronger or darker as the other gets weaker or lighter. However, there is a common pitfall that is shown in the example above.

While trying to create a gradient from light blue to white, a banding pattern has been introduced as the half-tone printing screens simulate the subtle tone changes across the image (above left). This banding can be avoided by adding noise into the gradient to disperse or dither the color, adding a more random pattern to the screen angles (above right).

tints

A tint is a color printed at a percentage of ten to 90 per cent of its full strength, and is created using half-tone dots of different sizes so that there is color dilution from the substrate.

tint books

Many tints are achievable with the standard process colors, either alone or in combination. These can be viewed in tint books that present swatches of the different tints. Tint books are printed on different stock varieties so that a designer can see how a tint will appear on different substrates, such as coated or uncoated. Ultimately, the best way to see how a tint works is through a test print (left) that shows exactly how each tint will appear on the desired stock.

multiple colored gradients

Many gradients feature a single or pair of colors, but multiple colors and patterns can also be used. In general, the same principles apply as with normal gradients as banding can occur with light colors, and strong colors can interfere with each other.

The illustrations below show the use of multicolored gradients as overlays to produce subtle visual effects rather than provide object fill. The effect they produce is in essence like changing the lighting conditions under which the photograph was taken. The gradients cool and warm different parts of the image. This is achieved by overlaying each of the three gradients in turn on to the base image (right). Notice how you can still detect the shape of the gradient, whether it is linear or circular.

original image

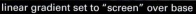

linear gradient

A linear gradient blends from one color to another in a series of vertical steps. The blend colors (here, white and blue) are controlled by sliders so that a designer can determine the emphasis of the blend. The default is halfway between two colors, but it can be altered with the sliders.

multiple colours

This gradient features multiple colors. The gradient sliders can be moved to make the transition from color to color sharper or more subtle.

radial gradient

A radial gradient creates a blend in a circle pattern so that it issues from a central point. This gradient can be controlled in the same way as a linear gradient to change the emphasis of gradient application, giving precise control to the designer.

linear gradient set to "screen" over base

multiple color gradient set to "lighten"

radial gradient overlaying base image

line weights

A design can feature a variety of different line weights for boxes, rules or other graphic interventions, but there are a few limitations to be aware of.

understanding line weights

The first variable to be considered is the measurement unit a line weight is specified in, as some software works in millimeters while desktop publishing programs often work in points. Most programs allow a designer to change the unit of measure so that work can be performed in a unified manner to minimize the potential risk of printing problems.

A designer also needs to be aware of the limitations of the printing process that mean a "hairline" (a default setting that is sometimes as thin as 0.125pt) is often too fine to print. The diagram below shows some potential line weight printing problems.

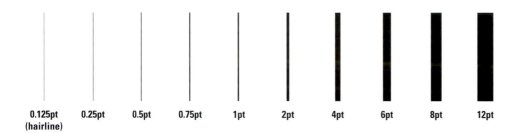

process lines
Producing a line in a solid process color generally provides an accurate print. Here even a hairline setting produces a solid, visible line.

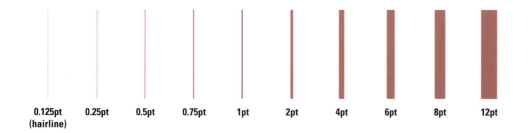

CMYK
Printing lines in a mixed-percentage color is less accurate as two screens are used to produce the color featuring half-tone dots at different sizes. Aligning these dots in a line such as an arrow causes visible problems.

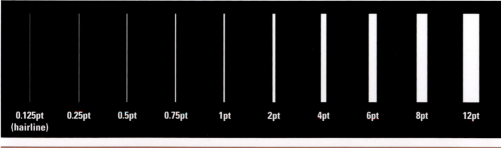

reversing out of a process color
Reversing a line out of a solid process color produces good results, but may have problems with fine lines due to dot gain.

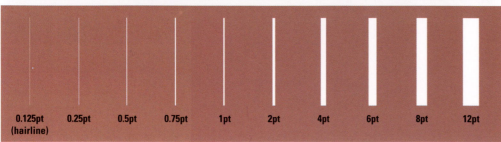

reversing out of CMYK
Reversing lines out of CMYK is less accurate due to potential color registration problems. For this reason fine lines can be difficult to produce in reverse.

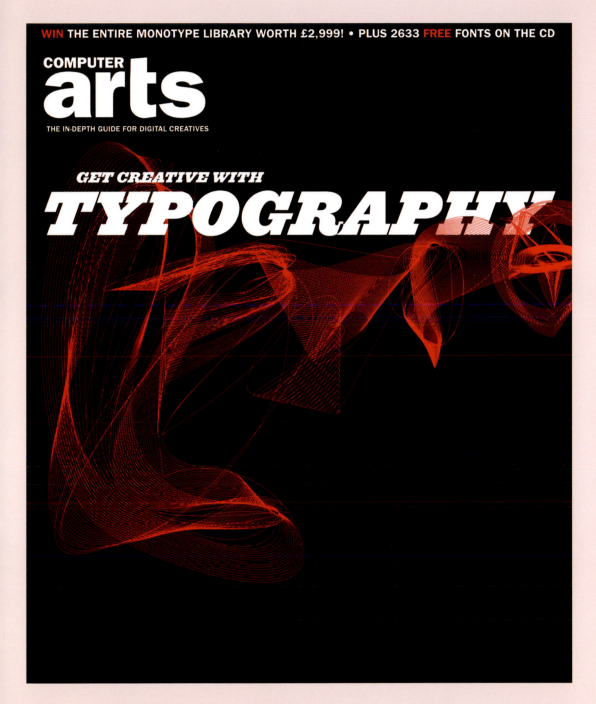

WIN THE ENTIRE MONOTYPE LIBRARY WORTH £2,999! • PLUS 2633 **FREE** FONTS ON THE CD

COMPUTER
arts
THE IN-DEPTH GUIDE FOR DIGITAL CREATIVES

GET CREATIVE WITH
TYPOGRAPHY

***Computer Arts* (left)**
Pictured is the cover of *Computer Arts* magazine created by Research Studios. It features a design that uses vector graphic lines to produce the word type. Due to the fineness of some of these lines, this was printed in a special process color.

London Calling (below)
This logo was created by Social Design and features the use of concentric rules of decreasing line weights to build up the letters within it.

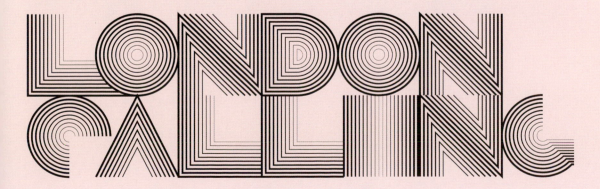

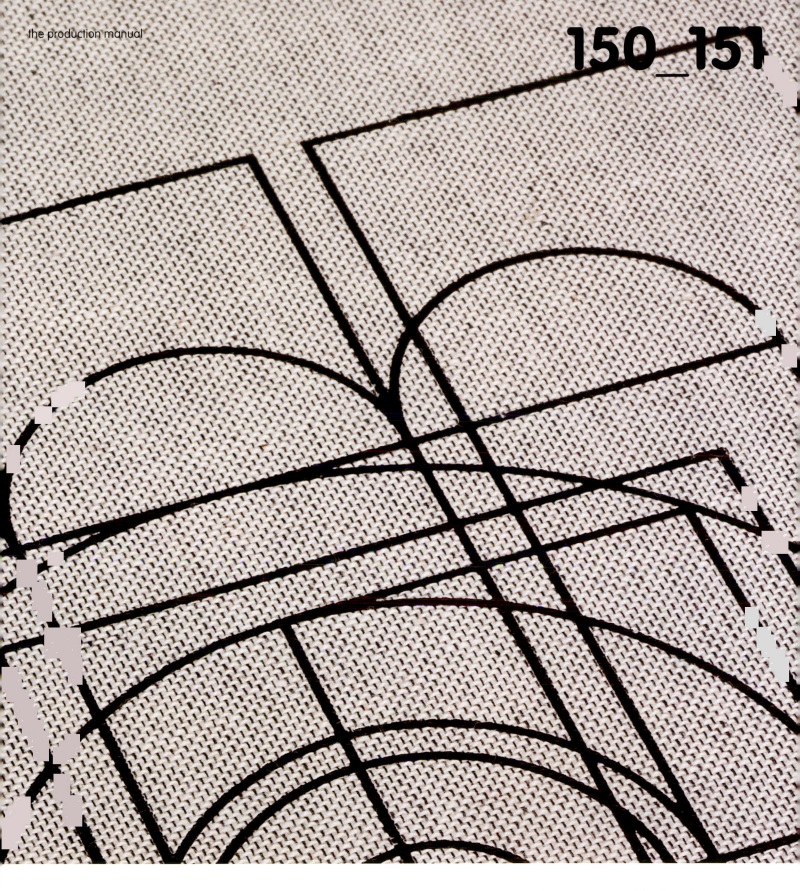

Not all line weights are equal in that they may reproduce differently on different stocks or with different printing processes. A laser printer or lithographic printing machine can print a finer line than is possible with screen printing or foil blocking, for example. Designers need to take the production method into account when creating a design so that it reproduces well.

A catalog created by Danish design agency Designbolaget for KUNSTEN Museum of Modern Art, Aalborg, for an interactive exhibition featuring artists Usman Hague, Tomás Saraceno and Joachim / ART+COM. The design features a fine line design, foil-stamped onto a cloth cover.

print processes

Printing is a process whereby ink or varnish from a printing plate is applied to a substrate with pressure. Modern printing technology also includes inkjet printing, whereby the ink is sprayed onto the substrate.

printing methods

There are four main processes used by the commercial printing industry: offset lithography, gravure, letterpress and silk screen. All of these differ in cost, production quality and production rate or volume.

lithography

Lithographic printing is a process whereby the inked image from a printing plate is transferred or offset on to a rubber blanket roller, which is then pressed against the substrate. Lithography uses a smooth printing plate and functions on the basis that oil and water repel each other. When the plate passes under the ink roller, non-image areas that have a water film repel the oily inks that stick to the image areas.

Lithography produces good photographic reproduction and fine linework on a variety of stocks. The printing plates are easy to prepare and high speeds are achievable, which helps make it a low-cost printing method.

Offset lithography is available in sheet-fed printing presses and continuous web presses. Sheet-fed presses are used for lower production runs, such as flyers, brochures and magazines, while web printing is used for high-volume print jobs, such as newspapers, magazines and reports.

lithography press

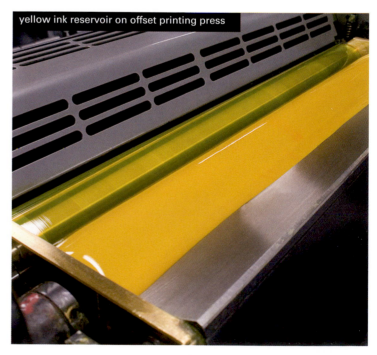

yellow ink reservoir on offset printing press

web printing

Web printing uses stock that is supplied on massive rolls rather than individual sheets. This allows for higher volume printing speeds and a lower production cost per unit for high-volume print jobs. Webs can be used with lithography, but more commonly with relief printing methods such as rotogravure and flexography as the plates are more durable. Due to the scale and cost of this production method, it is not suitable for low-volume print runs.

different printing applications will require different half-tone screens (Higher quality printing uses finer screen values)

Printing method	Lines per inch
Newsprint	85–110
Web offset	133
Standard sheet-fed offset	150
Fine quality	175–200

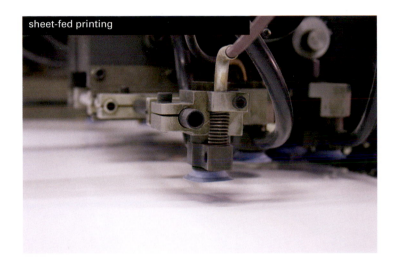

sheet-fed printing

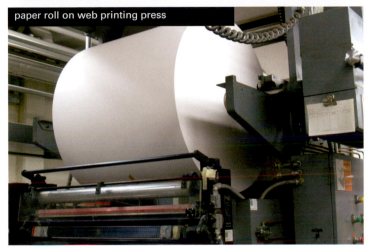

paper roll on web printing press

common problems with web and litho printing

The main drawbacks to offset lithography concern print run, as the cost benefits of the method are achieved with medium to long print runs. However, for high or very high print runs, image quality can start to suffer due to wear on the plate, so rotogravure is generally used instead.

Color control can be an issue due to problems with the ink/water balance on the plate and the presence of water can cause more absorbent substrates to distort. A dense ink film is also difficult to achieve.

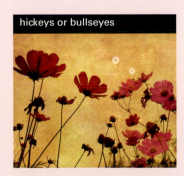

hickeys or bullseyes

Spots or other imperfections on the printed image caused by dried ink, dirt or other particles on the press can cause hickeys or bullseyes such as these above the flowers.

mis-registration

The misalignment of one or more of the printed images, perhaps due to the presence of water in the lithographic process, can distort the stock. Here mis-registration is noticeable by the blocks of yellow and red color.

setoff

Also called offset, this problem sees ink from one printed sheet unintentionally mark or transfer to the next sheet, such as the smudge over this woman's face.

color variation

Failure to maintain a constant and adequate ink/water balance on the printing plate can result in color variation, particularly over a long print run, which has caused banding in the landscape above.

movable typeimage

block type

letterpress

A method of relief printing whereby an inked, raised surface is pressed against a substrate. Letterpress was the first commercial printing method and the source of many printing methods. The raised surface that is inked for printing may be made from single type blocks, cast lines or engraved plates. Relief printing methods can be identified by the sharp and precise edges to letters and their heavier ink borders. Rotogravure is a more common commercial relief print process in which an image is engraved into a copper printing plate that is pressed directly against the substrate. Using a laser or diamond tool, small cells are engraved into the plate to hold the ink that will transfer to the stock, with a separate printing unit for each colour. Rotogravure is a high-speed printing process that can give the highest production volume and has the widest printing presses. Rotogravure is used for very large print runs.

Another method with which the image is carried by surface differences in the plate is flexography. This process creates a rubber relief of the image, which is inked and pressed against the substrate. Developed for printing packaging materials, the process was traditionally a lower quality reproduction method, but it now competes with rotogravure and lithography, particularly as it can print on a wider range of substrates due to the flexibility of its plate. Flexography is used for medium to large print runs.

Both rotogravure and flexography tend to use lower-viscosity inks than lithography, allowing for faster drying times.

Forme London calling cards (above)

These calling cards were created by and for Forme London print studio. They feature fonts from its letterpress archive and the words "comp" and "spools" refer to two terms frequently used in letterpress printing methods. A spool is used to collect type in a monotype keyboard, while comp is an abbreviation of compositor, the person that composes type to put on a page.

ink is applied to the screen that contains the image

ink is drawn through the screen and on to the substrate

the finished print job

Levi's (above)

This design, created by Kate Gibb and Rob Petrie for Levi's, features a tritone produced using a screen print to color different sections and highlight the clothing.

screen-printing

Screen-printing is a relatively low-volume printing method in which a viscous ink is passed through a screen—originally made from silk—that holds a design, on to a substrate. Although a relatively slow, low-volume and expensive printing method, screen-printing allows images to be applied to a wide range of substrates, including cloth, ceramics and metals, which are beyond the pale of other printing methods. The viscous inks allow specific colors to be applied and can also be used to create a raised surface that adds a tactile element to a design.

Wedding stationery (above)

Pictured above is a screen-printer printing wedding stationery that was created by The Gentle Group design studio.

on-press

Color can be adjusted on a printing press while a job is printing. This is normally done to achieve color consistency or to correct any color defects that arise during the printing process.

adjusting color

Color adjustments may be made on-press to account for color variation caused by changes in ink density or plate pressure. A printer makes color adjustments to ensure that the colors printing are the same as those on the color proof that is used as a reference and/or contract proof.

proof marking

A designer often needs to review a wet proof of a job and mark up where changes to the color are necessary. A designer or printer uses an eye glass to check color production against the control strips and uses the symbols below to accurately specify the changes required to print color, such as increasing or decreasing the intensity of the hue.

color checking, basic tools

To check the color of a job, a printed sheet is pulled from the press and checked using a color densitometer, a device that uses a light source and a photoelectric cell to measure optical density, or a spectrophotometer. The measurements obtained can be compared with those obtained from the color proof, a test strip, or a Pantone color swatch when special colors are printed. A printer also uses a loupe or eyeglass to check color registration.

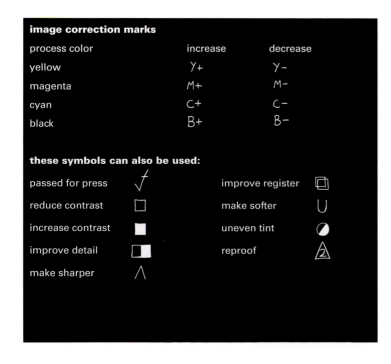

image correction marks

process color	increase	decrease
yellow	Y+	Y−
magenta	M+	M−
cyan	C+	C−
black	B+	B−

these symbols can also be used:

passed for press	✓	improve register	▢
reduce contrast	▢	make softer	U
increase contrast	◼	uneven tint	◑
improve detail	◨	reproof	△2
make sharper	∧		

densitometer

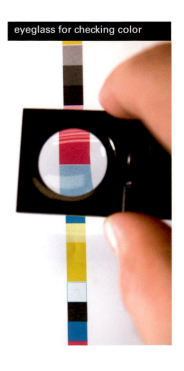

eyeglass for checking color

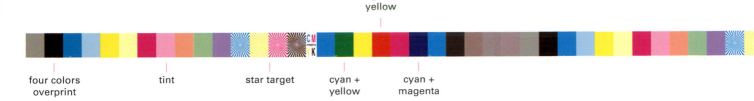

magenta +
yellow

four colors
overprint

tint

star target

cyan +
yellow

cyan +
magenta

striker bar

A printed sheet has a striker bar containing a series of predefined colors printed along its edge for color checking. The bar includes additive primaries, subtractive primaries and overprints, as shown above, while star targets allow a printer to test for dot gain. Even though a densitometer may say a job is printing accurately, whether a job needs more or less color running is a judgment that requires human instinct.

the press

A modern lithographic printing press can control the color density/plate pressure on the stock, which allows a printer to adjust in increments the balance of each color being printed. A printer regularly pulls sheets from the press during printing to check against the color proof. Readjustments can be made if necessary, using the controls (below left) that change ink flow of different vertical slithers directly onto the stock. The example below has an exaggerated color alteration of a single slither to show how an alteration affects all the pages it prints.

the imposed sheet

The way a sheet is imposed affects how much color can be altered while printing. In the example below, eight pages are printed to view, which means that altering a vertical strip on a lower page will have an impact on a higher page. When all colors are similar, this is not usually problematic. However, isolated patches of solid color, such as a black square, can be more difficult to alter. Running a bouncer behind the color can reduce this problem, as it would use two colors, meaning that any individual color has to do less work.

the printing press controls

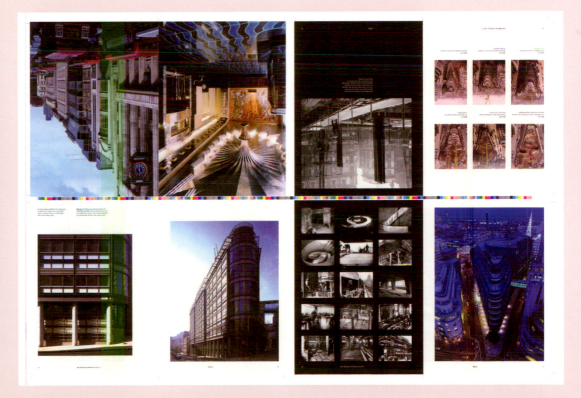

A designer may be able to plan a publication to group strong colors together in vertical slithers, such as the black in the example, so alterations to the color are applied to the whole slither. However, it is more common to find a solid color above a very light page that minimizes the amount that one color can be pushed, which is why color correction issues must be resolved at the proofing stage (see page 128—129) before going to press. Bending a color to remove a cast will alter the color reproduction of other elements on the printed sheet, which needs to be borne in mind, as many jobs are printed with eight or 16 pages to view.

paper

A designer can choose from a wide range of stocks on which to print a job. Stocks differ by size, color, texture, composition, printability and various other factors that need to be taken into account during the selection process.

paper qualities

Paper weight, grain and paper direction are key physical characteristics to consider when selecting and using a stock for a publication. Different stocks can have a profound impact on the feel of a design due to their tactile qualities. A coated stock has a very different feel or touch to an uncoated stock, or coarser stocks such as those that can be made from recycled paper.

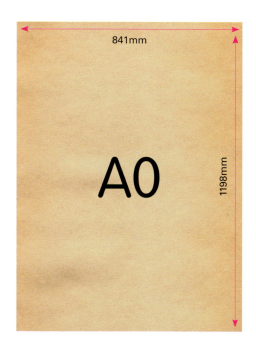

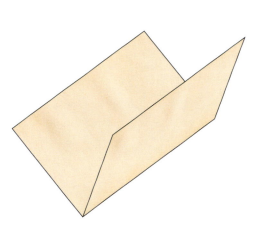

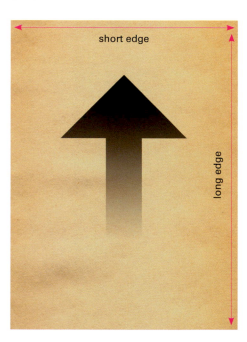

paper weight
Basis Weight in the US (Bond, Book, Index, Cover, Tag, Points, Offset), and GSM (or grams per square meter) in the UK, are part of a paper specification based on the weight of the paper.

paper grain
Paper produced on a paper machine has a grain because the fibers from which it is made line up during the manufacturing process in the direction that it passes through the paper-making machine. The grain is the direction in which most of the fibers lay. This characteristic means that paper is easier to fold, bend or tear along its grain direction.

direction
The direction of fibers in paper for laser printers, such as those found in offices, typically has a grain that runs parallel to the long side of the paper to allow it to pass more easily through the printer.

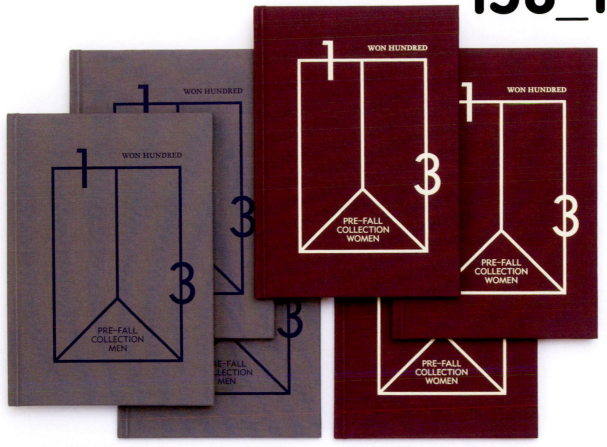

Won Hundred

Pictured are the covers of lookbooks created by Danish design agency Designbolaget for fashion brand Won Hundred. They show how using different print processes and different stocks can produce striking results. The Pre-Fall 13 lookbook (above) features a foil stamp on a cloth cover, while the Spring-Summer 13 cover (below) features a silk-screen on recycled paper.

paper types and print quality

Many different types of paper stock are available to the designer. For example, this book prints on two different stocks: a matt art, and a gloss art. In addition to adding different colors and textures to a print job, these also have different printability characteristics and cost. Paper characteristics that affect printability include its smoothness, absorbency, opacity and ink holdout. The table opposite is designed as a quick guide to the characteristics of some main paper types.

smoothness

The smooth surface of these stocks is obtained through the use of filler elements that may be polished with calendering rollers. They are typically glossy as well.

absorbency

Stocks have different absorbency levels, which is the degree to which the ink penetrates it. Printing inks tend to dry quicker on absorbent stocks, but absorbency may cause problems such as dot gain.

opacity

Opacity is used to describe the extent to which whatever is printed on one side of a sheet shows through and is visible on the other. High-opacity papers have no show-through.

ink holdout

This is the degree to which a stock resists ink penetration due to its relative lack of absorbency. Coated stocks may be particularly prone to ink holdout as the ink sits on the surface, which in turn increases drying time.

This creation by Phage is printed on a decorative stock. Designers today have a choice of paper stocks that is wider than ever before.

type of paper	notes	primary uses	secondary uses	effect
Uncoated	An uncoated (non-glossy) stock that feels thick and substantial in your hands, and is suitable for full-color printing.	To add texture to publications such as annual reports.	Stationery and flyers.	A textured stock with a rough or matt surface.
Art	A high-quality paper with a clay coating on both sides to give a good printing surface, especially for half-tones, where definition and detail are important.	Color printing and magazines.	Flyers, calendars and brochures.	A glossy, high brightness surface that is smooth to the touch.
Artboard	Uncoated board.	Cover stock.	Flyers and packaging.	A stiff stock.
Cartridge	A thick white paper. Ink and pencil drawings are particularly well produced on this.	Stationery and annual reports.	Mail shots.	A stiff feel, available in several colors.
Cast coated	Wet-coated paper is pressed (cast) against a hot, polished metal drum to obtain a high gloss.	Magazines and brochures.	Promotional material.	A smooth, glossy surface.
Chromo	A waterproof coating is applied to one side of the paper to allow for embossing and varnishing processes.	Labels, wrappings and covers.	Applications where only one side has to be printed.	Clay coated on one side; can be glossy or matt.
Flock	Paper coated with flock; very fine woollen surface. Used for decorative covers. Other coatings might be refuse or vegetable fiber dust to give a velvety or cloth-like appearance.	Decorative covers.	Packaging.	A textured, decorative surface.
Greyboard	Lined or unlined board made from waste paper.	Packaging material.	Covers.	Rough texture, good bulk and gray color.
Mechanical	Produced using wood pulp and acidic chemicals, this paper is suitable for short-term use as it yellows and fades quickly.	Newspapers and directories.	Magazines, inserts, flyers, coupons and books.	Higher brightness and smoothness than newsprint, but uncoated and matt.
NCR (No Carbon Required)	A carbonless coating to make duplicate copies. Available in two- to six-part.	Forms and purchase orders.	Receipts.	The application of pressure produces an impression on subsequent parts.
Newsprint	Made primarily of mechanically-ground wood pulp, this is the cheapest paper that can withstand standard printing processes. It has a short life-span and reproduces color poorly.	Newspapers and comics.	Low-quality printing.	Absorbent, comparatively rough surface.
Plike	A rubberised substrate.	Cover stock.	Flyers.	Rubbery texture.
Uncoated woodfree	This paper is the most commonly used in non-commercial printing. Most stationery and printer/photocopier paper falls into this category, although some offset grades are also used for general commercial printing.	Office paper (printer and photocopy paper, stationery).	Forms and envelopes.	A white paper with a slightly rough, non-glossy surface.

Neat Confections

Pictured is packaging created by Mexican agency Anagrama for a branding of pastry shop Neat Confections that feature the use of a highly reflective silver stock, which becomes an important part of an identity. Perfection is the main character in the branding proposal. The quality of the product is reflected. The silver chrome surfaces in every piece of packaging provides a pureness that reflects the quality of the natural ingredients of the pastry products while allowing them to stand out when the packaging is opened.

NEAT CONFECTIONS

GALLETAS DE MANTEQUILLA

TRIBUTO A:

CAFÉ MASALA

Cálido, especiado, ahumado, e intenso, la mezcla
de especias logra un fragante y único sabor.

CONT. NET. 130 GR.

NEAT CONFECTIONS

GALLETAS DE MANTEQUILLA

TRIBUTO A:

TÉ MATCHA

El suave carácter lácteo de la mantequilla francesa se
transforma ante la sutil calidez herbal y tostada del té
verde japonés.

CONT. NET. 130 GR.

sustainability

Environmental sustainability is now a key concern for both clients and final consumers, in order to reduce the impact of production and consumption on the Earth's resources. Companies actively engage in efforts to reduce their environmental impact by reducing the use of materials and changing their purchasing habits to utilize products and services that have a lower impact.

sustainable printing

For several years now, sustainable printing has been a growing concept in the printing industry and many printers specialize in offering environmentally friendly services to cater for this growing niche of consumers that want to make a difference.

This effort goes beyond the use of recycled paper to include developments such as chlorine-free paper, "waterless" technology (to avoid the use of isopropanol alcohol, one of the printing industry's major pollutants), and environmentally friendly inks made from linseed and soya vegetable oils (to replace traditional printing inks). Vegetable inks are less toxic and easier to remove than traditional pigment transfer vehicles, which eases the de-inking process during paper recycling, according to the National Non-Food Crops Centre.

Graphic designers have a huge role to play in this change in behavior, as they typically specify the print job. Design Anarchy details simple changes that designers can make to reduce the environmental impact of printing. These include reducing point size, sending PDFs instead of print-outs and obtaining print estimates at the start of a job where there may be cost-saving flexibility related to format size.

Print customers can do their part by specifying the use of recycled and/or environmentally friendly products, and by minimizing the use of foils, varnishes, specials and other treatments that perhaps have higher resource usage. They can also provide more precise job specifications—indeed, as technologies such as print-on-demand become more common it becomes possible to specify more exacting print runs that obviate the need to produce extras, saving materials as well as transportation and storage costs.

An environmental consciousness is often thought to imply a trade-off in terms of quality, which many print industry clients are not prepared to accept. However, many environmentally friendly products and technologies produce high-quality results, and it is worth remembering how recycled paper has evolved from a poor-quality product to something much better today.

environment ISO 14000 accredited

ISO 14000 is an international standard that certifies that a company follows environmental management standards to minimize the negative impact its operations have on the environment, in addition to compliance with all relevant local and international legislation.

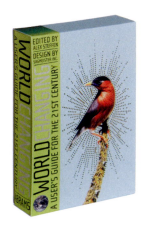 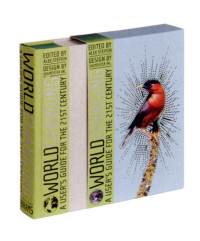 

World (left)

Pictured is *World*, a publication reporting on developments in science, engineering, architecture, business, and politics that was created by Sagmeister Inc. for publisher Harry N Abrams Inc. It features a die-cut slipcase that will change color over time if left in direct light.

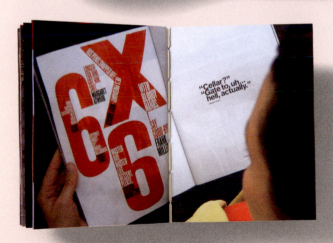

Frost* (above)
The new mini *Frost** book, produced by Frost* Design, Sydney, showcases work in progress from its first year in business, and is printed with vegetable inks.

case study:

Park House

NB Studio, UK

NB Studio was tasked with creating a brand identity for a striking new commercial development in London. The brief was to create a brand identity that would reflect the quality, ambition and presence of the development, and that would be used on a range of marketing collateral to help attract investors. The results included an eye-catching and unusual piece of print production.

NB Studio had to produce a design solution that was a flexible brand identity and that would be appropriate for multiple audiences. "A mixed-use development like this is challenging as it has a diverse audience: Park House sits on Oxford Street (where you are essentially selling to retailers) and in Mayfair (where you are aiming for commercial office and residential clients)".

The solution was a set of visual identity elements inspired by the building's striking design, and holding all the separate elements together. The concentric circles in the design link together as a metaphor for bringing the different elements of the building development and diverse mix of investors together. The circle theme is flexible enough to be propagated throughout the design intervention, from a bespoke typeface, a sculpture, and even the building's own brand of bottled water.

"We looked to the lines and flowing forms of the building and the sculptural work by Walter Bailey that was commissioned for the lobbies. We'd been given Walter's sketches and seen how he uses a chainsaw and blowtorch to create his impressive wooden sculptures," says Jamie Breach.

From working with concentric circles to create a brand identity, it was a short step to extrapolate this to a bespoke typeface. "While working with concentric circles in fine line, we experimented with typographic form and this gave us a unique display typeface to use when marketing the building. This gave us a valuable element to our visual toolkit and meant that design decisions became easier," he said.

Park House cover (facing page)
Pictured is the wooden cover for the Park House brochure box. Produced from MDF, the box has an oak veneer that is laser etched and screen printed, and has a magnetic steel closure.

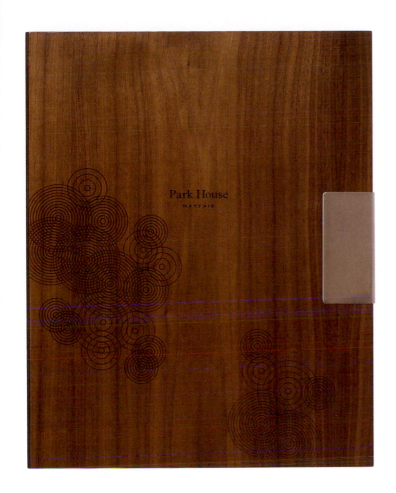

"A mixed-use development like this is challenging as it has a diverse audience: Park House sits on Oxford Street (where you are essentially selling to retailers) and in Mayfair (where you are aiming for commercial office and residential clients)"

Jamie Breach, NB Studio

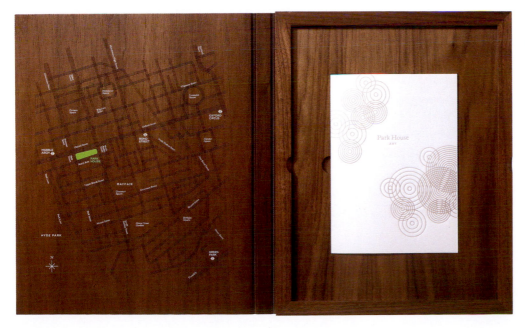

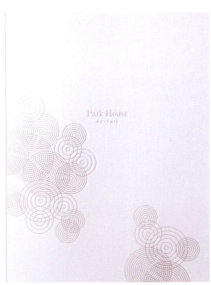

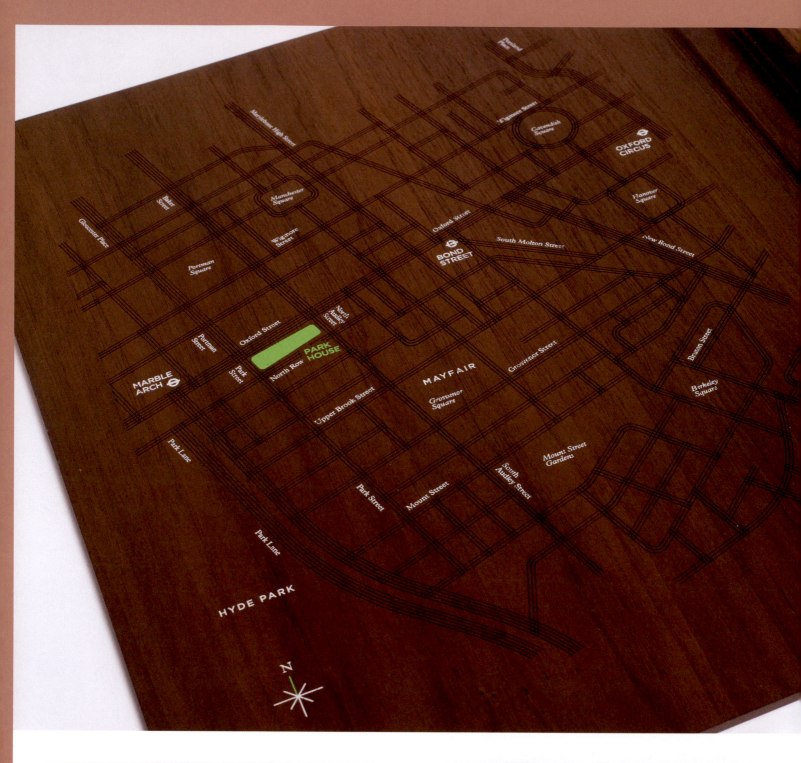

MARLYEBONE HIGH STREET

Wigmore Street

CAVENDISH SQUARE

OXFORD CIRCUS

Baker Street

MANCHESTER SQUARE

HANOVER SQUARE

GLOUCESTER PLACE

Wigmore Street

Oxford Street

SOUTH MOLTON STREET

NEW BOND STREET

PORTMAN SQUARE

BOND STREET

Oxford Street

North Audley Street

PARK HOUSE

Bruton Street

PORTMAN STREET

MARBLE ARCH

Park Street

North Row

MAYFAIR

Grosvenor Street

BERKELEY SQUARE

Upper Brook Street

GROSVENOR SQUARE

PARK LANE

Mount Street Gardens

Park Street

Mount Street

South Audley Street

PARK LANE

HYDE PARK

N

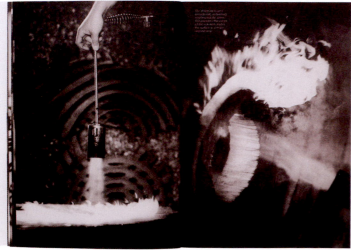

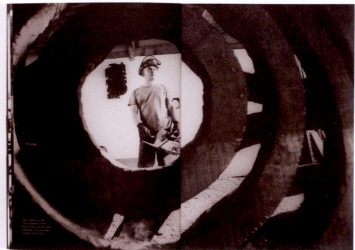

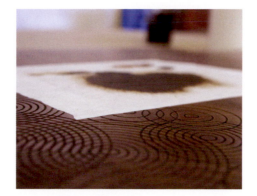

The marketing materials reflect the attention to detail, high production values and unique materials that form part of the development's design story. The marketing pack comprises a wooden box containing a brochure and art book. The box is laser etched and screen printed and is fitted with a magnetic closure. The brochure used process colors and three special colors and has a foil blocked cover, while the art book uses black and four special colors with a foil-blocked cover.

"The brochure and other contents of the box were used as a selling tool, aimed at the commercial market in Mayfair. So, in short, we were talking to people who were about to spend a lot of money and needed cues and reassurances that Park House was a sound business decision as well as a bold statement. The wooden box was inspired by the luxurious materials used in the development itself. We worked hard to choose materials that would convey the craftsmanship and design credentials that Land Securities and their architects achieved with Park House," he says.

Pictured above are a series of images showing the application of the laser etching and screen printing to the oak veneer of the Park House brochure box.

chapter six
finishing

This chapter covers a wide range of processes that provide the finishing touches to a design once the substrate has been printed. These processes include die cutting, binding, special print techniques, laminates, varnishes, folding, foil blocking, and screen-printing, all of which can transform an ordinary-looking piece into something much more interesting and dynamic.

Finishing processes can add decorative elements to a printed piece, such as the shimmer of a foil block or the texture of an emboss. They can also provide added functionality to a design and even be a constituent part of a publication's format, for example, a matt lamination to protect a substrate, making it last longer.

Although the application of print-finishing techniques signals the end of the production process, these techniques should not be considered as afterthoughts, but as an integral part of a design at the planning stage.

The Arts and Crafts Movement (facing page)
This book cover was created by Webb & Webb design studio for publisher, Phaidon. It features a deep emboss of a design by Victorian fabric designer, William Morris, for Windrush wallpaper.

special techniques

Special techniques, such as specialty printing, add an extra touch of value-adding excitement to a design.

specialty printing

Certain print techniques allow a designer to produce something different to what standard offset lithography can produce. These techniques may be more expensive due to the additional set-up time required and lower volumes they can produce, but they can certainly help lift and add value to a design.

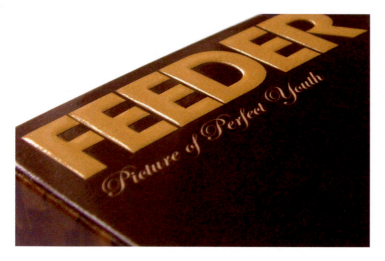

embossing

An emboss uses a metal die holding an image to stamp the stock from below and leave an impression. As the design has to push through the stock, designs are usually slightly oversized, with heavier lines and extra space inserted between letters. Thinner stocks can hold more detail than thicker stocks, but intricate designs do not reproduce well. Thicker stocks generally require thicker lines as the image has to press through more fibers. Coated stocks hold detail well, but the coating may crack, meaning that uncoated stock is better for deep embossing. Foil can also be added to give coloration, such as the gold foil block on Feeder's "Picture of Perfect Youth" CD package created by Social Design, above. Copper and brass dies are more durable and should be used for high print run jobs, those using thick or abrasive stocks and those where the design is more detailed.

debossing

A deboss uses a metal dye containing a design, which is stamped from above on to stock to leave an indentation. Debossing works in the same way as embossing and the same stock caliper considerations apply. While embossing tends to create highlights due to the raised surface, debossing creates shadows of the indented surface as can be seen in this brochure created by Third Eye Design for Scottish cashmere manufacturer BEGG. The shadowing makes the typeface characters appear as though they have been carved in marble due to the white-on-white effect produced, which is timeless and elegant.

Monsters Ink (opposite)

Pictured above are invites to a Halloween party, created by and for NB: Studio. They feature illustrations of monsters by James Graham that were screen-printed in luminous ink on to black stock to give a dark, contrasting feel to the piece that glows in the dark.

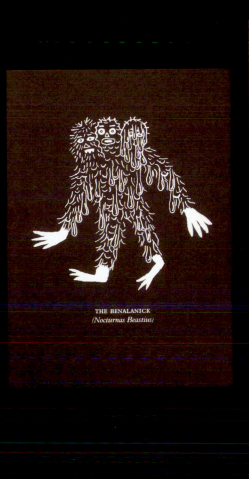

THE BENALANICK
(Nocturnas Beastius)

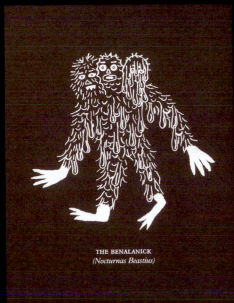

THE BENALANICK
(Nocturnas Beastius)

THE BENALANICK
(Nocturnas Beastius)

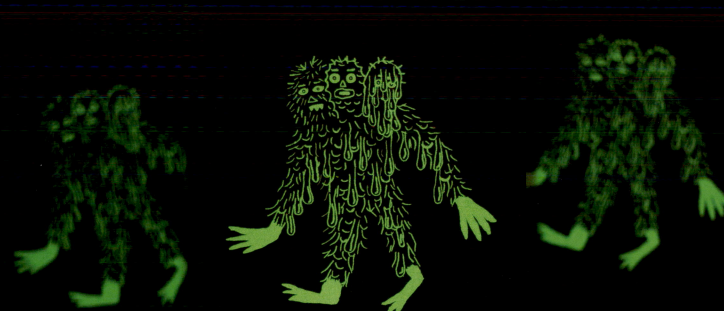

Fedrigoni
An example of embossed foil, used by Phage for the annual promotional calendar of Italian luxury paper manufacturer Fedrigoni. By showcasing different stocks from Fedrigoni's luxury range, the design promoted their product to a design-aware audience.

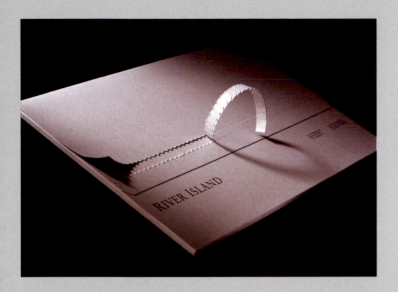

perforation

Perforation, or perf cutting, is a process that creates a cut-out area in a substrate to weaken it so that it can be detached. Pictured above is a mailout package created by Third Eye Design for fashion retailer River Island, which features perforated stock.

duplexing

Duplexing is the bonding of two stocks to form a single substrate with different colours or textures on each side. Pictured above is an invite created by SEA for paper merchant GF Smith, which features a duplexed substrate to highlight two of the client's paper stocks.

foils

Foil blocking is a process whereby a colored foil is pressed on to a substrate via a heated die. Also called foil stamp, heat stamp or foil emboss, the process allows a designer to add a shiny finish to specific design elements such as title text, as shown on the copper foil block pictured above, created for Thai real estate development Real by Anagrama.

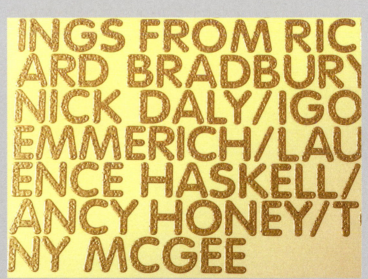

thermography

Thermography is a print-finishing process that produces raised lettering by fusing thermographic powder to a design in an oven. Pictured above is a Christmas card created by design studio SEA for the Lisa Pritchard Agency. The text has been thermographically printed to give the letters a raised, bubbly, mottled surface that is highly visible and very tactile.

cutting methods

Die, laser and kiss cutting are all methods for removing portions of stock to create different shapes.

die cutting

Die cutting uses a steel die to cut away a specified section of a design. It is mainly used to add a decorative element to a print job and enhance the visual performance of the piece.

Peter and Paul (left)
This business card was created by and for Peter and Paul design studio. The card is used by both Peter and Paul as it features the name of one partner on one side and the other on the reverse. Additional information is embossed into the mottled black stock to create a tactile and memorable identity.

Sally Dernie (below)
Stationery created by Phage as part of an identity for interior designer Sally Dernie, featuring a die-cut scalloped edge.

laser cutting

Laser cutting uses a laser to cut shapes into the stock rather than use a metal tool. Laser cutting can produce more intricate cut-outs with a cleaner edge than a steel die, although the heat of the laser burns the cut edge. Faster set-up times mean faster job turnaround.

Laser-cut card (left)

An example of laser cutting created by Blok Design as part of an identity for Laboratorio Para La Ciudad, an organization founded by the Mexico City government to cultivate and elevate the city's creativity and innovation. Notice how the cut edges have been burnt by the laser, adding an interesting additional visual aspect.

kiss cutting

This is a die-cutting method often used with self-adhesive substrates, whereby the face stock is die cut but not its backing sheet, to facilitate the easy removal of the cut stock. Kiss cutting is commonly seen in the production of stickers. The artwork supplied for kiss cutting needs to include a cutter guide as shown below right. A common form of kiss cut is called Crack-Back, which is a brand produced by Fasson.

Kiss-cut card

An example of kiss cutting created by Blok Design as part of an identity for Laboratorio Para La Ciudad, and used here to create self-adhesive stickers.

Ruinart
Pictured is an invitation created by Clormann Design for Ruinart, the world's oldest champagne house, for an event to launch a new product. The design of the invitation was derived from the look of the limited edition packaging for the product created by Scottish artist Georgia Russell for the Blanc de Blancs collection in lasercut metal. Clormann reproduced the design in paper stock via laser cutting and a hot foil stamp.

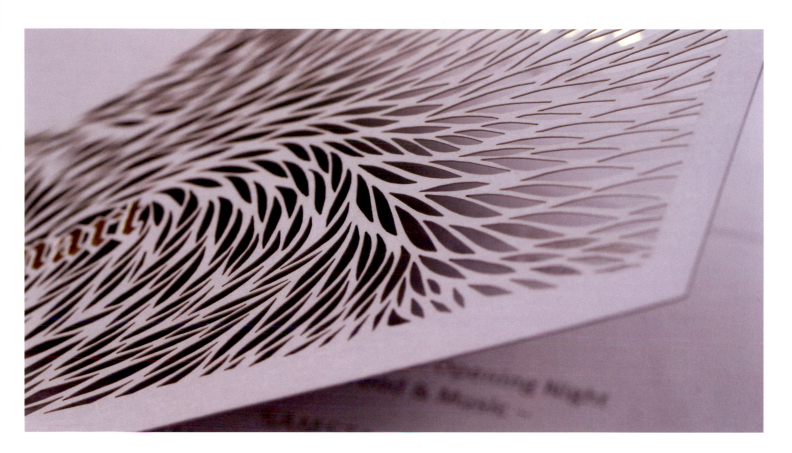

laminates and varnishes

Laminates and varnishes are print finishes applied to the printed job to add a finishing touch to the surface.

laminate types

A laminate is a layer of plastic coating that is heat-sealed on to the stock to produce a smooth and impervious finish, and to provide a protective layer to cover stock. A varnish is a colorless coating, applied to a printed piece to protect it from wear or smudging, and to enhance the visual appearance of the design or elements within it, such as a spot varnish.

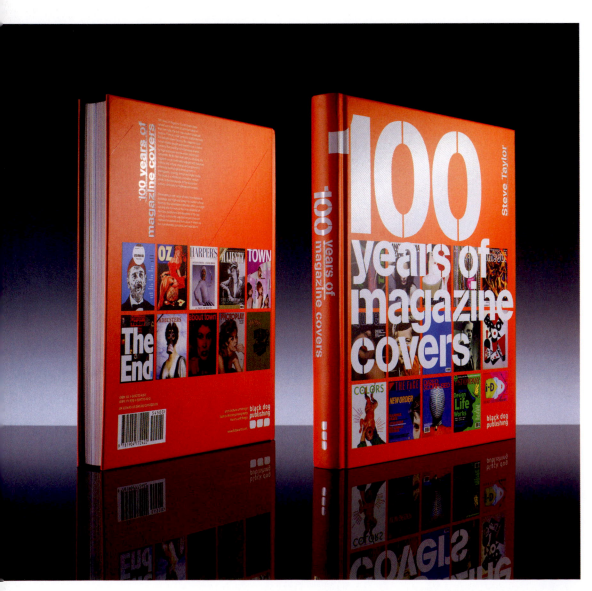

100 Years of Magazine Covers (left)
Pictured is *100 Years of Magazine Covers*, a book written by Steve Taylor and designed by Research Studios for Black Dog Publishing. It features a spot UV gloss on the cover and round-back binding to add a special touch.

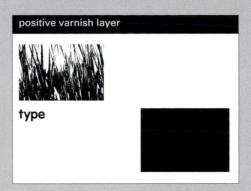

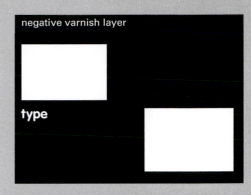

Pictured above is a schematic of the artwork that is to receive a varnish.

This image shows the file for a positive varnish application in which the images will receive the varnish (the grass stalks).

This image shows the negative varnish file in which the non-image areas will receive the varnish and the pictures will remain untouched.

supplying artwork for a laminate or varnish

Any part of a printed surface can have a spot varnish or laminate applied. To achieve this, a designer must send a separate file to show exactly where it will be placed. The file contains the artwork with the spot varnish or laminate design presented in black, as it will run as a solid color without any screening, while all other areas are white. Varnishes and laminates can be applied in different ways to produce a variety of effects.

For example, a positive varnish could be applied to the page above to cover the text and images. Conversely, a negative varnish could be applied where there are unprinted areas. Varnish can be used to enhance elements printed on to a matt stock. If printing on a high-gloss stock, the application of a matt varnish would take the sheen off the selected areas, subduing them and allowing the unvarnished area to shine and be the focal point. Remember that everything black will be varnished or laminated and everything white will not be.

types of varnish

gloss

Colors appear richer and more vivid when printed with a gloss varnish, so photographs appear sharper and more saturated. For this reason, a gloss finish is often used for brochures or other photographic publications.

matt (or dull)

The opposite of a gloss varnish, a matt coating will soften the appearance of a printed image. It will also make text easier to read as it diffuses light, thus reducing glare.

neutral

The application of a basic, almost invisible, coating that seals the printing ink without affecting the appearance of the job. It is often used to accelerate the drying of fast turnaround print jobs (such as leaflets) on matt and satin papers, on which inks dry more slowly.

pearlescent

A varnish that subtly reflects myriad colors to give a luxurious effect.

satin (or silk)

This coating tends to represent a midway point between gloss and matt varnishes.

textured spot UV

Textures can be applied to a design through the use of a spot UV. The textures that can be obtained are sandpaper, leather, crocodile skin and raised.

UV varnish

An ultraviolet varnish can be applied to printed paper and dried by exposure to UV radiation in order to create a coating that is glossier than any other. A printed page with this varnish will feel shiny and slightly sticky. UV varnish can be applied all over a publication (full-bleed UV) or to certain parts of a design (spot UV).

types of laminate

matt

A matt laminate helps diffuse light and reduce glare to increase the readability of text-heavy designs.

satin

This laminate provides a finish that is between matt and gloss. It provides some highlight, but is not as flat as matt.

gloss

A highly reflective laminate that is used to enhance the appearance of graphic elements and photographs on covers as it increases color saturation.

sand

A laminate that creates a subtle sand grain within a design.

leather

A laminate that gives a subtle leather texture to a design.

folding and trimming

Folding encompasses a range of different methods for turning a printed sheet into a more compact form or signature.

types of fold
The majority of folding techniques make use of the basic valley and mountain folds to create a series of peaks and troughs.

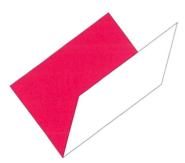

valley fold
Held horizontally, a valley fold has a central crease at the bottom with the panels rising upwards to form the sides.

mountain fold
Held horizontally, a mountain fold has a central crease at the top with the panels falling downwards.

NB: Studio card
Pictured above is a Christmas card created by and for design studio, NB: Studio, which features a series of box-step folds through which the different panels increase and decrease in size.

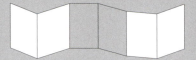

front / back accordion fold With three parallel folds, the two-panel outer wings fold into and out of the center. The double-panel center serves as the cover.

harmonica self-cover folder An accordion fold where the first two panels form a cover that the other panels fold into. The first two panels need to be larger than the others.

mock book fold Essentially an accordion fold where the penultimate two panels form a cover that the other panels fold into to create a book.

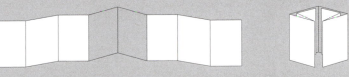

double gatefold The gatefold has three panels that fold in towards the center of the publication.

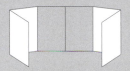

front / back gatefold An extra double panel that folds inside the front and / or back panel.

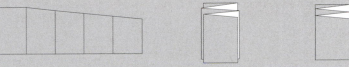

incline tab The stock top is cut away at an incline and accordion folded to present panels of increasing size from front to back.

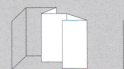

triple parallel fold Parallel folds creating a section that nests within the cover panels with a front opening. May be used for maps.

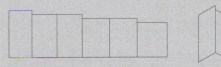

tab fold The stock top is cut away horizontally and accordion folded so that each pair of panels decreases in size from the full-size panel.

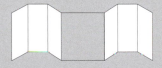

back / front folder Wings either side of the central panel have a double parallel fold so that they can fold around and cover both sides of the central panel.

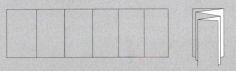

ascending folder The stock is accordion folded with increasing widths between folds so that each panel increases in size from front to back.

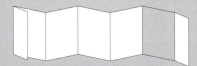

half cover from behind An accordion fold where the penultimate panel forms a back cover that the other panels fold into to create a book, but the half-size end panel folds around the book from behind to cover the front, together with the half-size first panel.

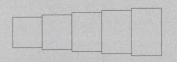
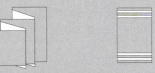

staggered folder design Stock is cut away horizontally from top and bottom to make each successive panel smaller than its predecessor and accordion folded.

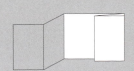

duelling z-fold Z-fold wings fold into the center panel and meet in the middle.

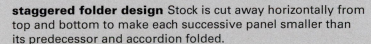
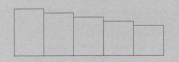

boxed step Stock top is cut away so that each panel decreases in size from the full-size panel. Accordion folded.

trimming and guillotining

Once a job has been printed, it proceeds to the finishing stage to undergo processes such as trimming, whereby excess stock is cut away from the design to produce the final format. While trimming may fall outside a designer's brief, discussing the trimming requirements with the printer or finishing firm may provide useful information that can be included within the design.

cutter draw

A trimming machine has a cutter, which is placed under the trim marks made by the designer. The printed pages are held secure and the blade descends under high pressure through the substrate to make the cut.

As there is usually a large number of sheets being cut, a cutter blade has a tendency to slide forward as it passes through the block. This may cause bowing in the block of stock as it is securely anchored at either edge. This is more of an issue with lighter stocks.

NB: Studio Christmas card (above)
Pictured is a Christmas card created by and for NB: Studio that features pages of different sizes that are folded and stitched together so that when the item is opened and the cover folded back on itself, they produce an extraordinary Christmas tree effect.

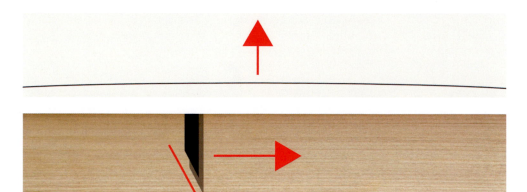

The stock pile bows upwards in the middle as it is securely held.

The cutter blade tends to slide forward as it cuts through a pile of stock.

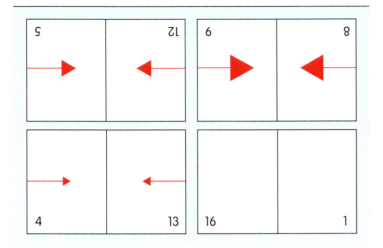

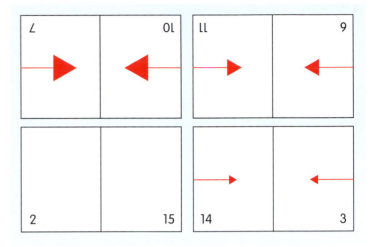

amending artwork to compensate for creep

Books are typically made of sections of folded pages that nest within each other and are bound together. As such, they can be subject to creep, a process whereby the inner pages extend beyond the outer pages, particularly with thicker stocks. However, a publication can be designed to take account of potential creep problems.

Modern print finishing workshops often feature guillotines that have a computer-controlled system to ensure trim consistency and accuracy.

High-print-run books and magazines may be trimmed on a three-knife trimmer, a cutting machine that trims all three edges in two cuts. The fore-edge knife makes the first cut and then the other two knives simultaneously cut the head and tail.

A guillotine is a single-knife cutter with a heavy blade that descends between vertical runners. A guillotine has a table on which the material to be cut is piled; a movable back gauge or fence, which is perpendicular to the table and against which the back edge of the pile rests; a clamp or press beam that compresses and secures the front edge of the pile that is to be cut; and a cutter. Modern cutters feature automatic spacing that causes the back gauge to move a pre-determined distance following each cut. For safety reasons, controls are designed to require both hands to be used to activate cutting operations.

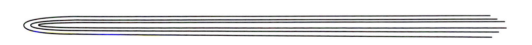

This illustration shows how the nesting of the pages in a section can result in the projection of excess paper at the trim edge.

over-runs and quantities

Once a job has been printed, it is delivered to a client or sent to a print finisher if further finishing processes are required. If the print order was for 1,000 copies, you would expect 1,000 to be delivered, but this does not always happen as many copies go to waste while a printing press is being run up, getting the colors correct and so on. If a job is to be sent to a finishing house for spot UV printing, die cutting or foiling, a printer usually prints more copies to allow for the wastage at the finishing house as they set up their equipment.

A printer may print overs (extra copies for your files) depending upon your relationship with the firm, but unless you specifically ask for 1,000 copies as a minimum, you may get fewer delivered as the 1,000 printed copies will be depleted due to the wastage from the various processes. A printer will not restart the press for a missing 50 copies and legally, they do not have to, so the best option is to speak with the printer and be explicit about how many copies are needed.

binding

Binding literally brings a job together. But in addition to this key utilitarian role, the binding method has visual and usability roles.

Binding

Binding is a process through which the various pages that comprise a job are securely held together so that they function as a publication. Different types of binding are available that serve different demands and impact the durability of the publication. Over and above holding the pages together, a binding can add to the narrative of the material it contains and also act as a visual indication of quality, due to the added attention to detail and cost that some binding techniques entail.

Many different types of binding are available and they all have different durability, aesthetics, costs and functional characteristics, as shown on the opposite page.

Anagarama (below)

Pictured below is a document wallet created as part of a branding project created by Anagrama for The Yachtsetter, a service that provides yacht and cabin rentals in addition to a clothing line and other accessories. The brand explores the combination of elegance and fun, finding its inspiration in nautical language and regattas. The function of the document wallet is to hold and store documents together, and Anagrama has created a closure mechanism that binds the wallet while reflecting both the rigging and pendants of the sailing world.

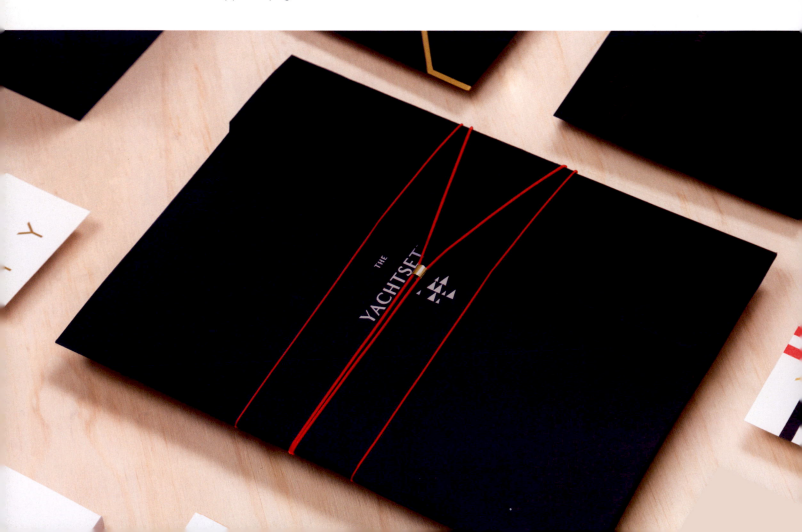

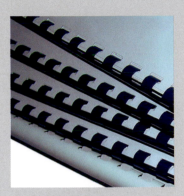

comb binding
A spine (comb) of plastic rings that bind and allow a document to open flat.

spiral binding
A spiral of metal wire that winds through punched holes allowing the publication to open flat.

wiro binding
A spine of metal (wiro) rings that bind and allow a document to open flat.

open bind
A book bound without a cover to leave an exposed spine.

belly band
A printed band that wraps around a publication, typically used with magazines.

singer stitch
A binding method whereby the pages are sewn together with one continual thread.

elastic bands
An informal binding whereby an elastic band holds the pages together and nestles in the center fold.

clips and bolts
A fastening device that holds loose pages together. This usually requires the insertion of a punched or drilled hole for the bolt or clip to pass through.

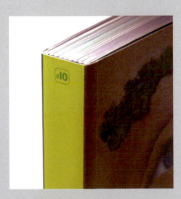

perfect bound
The backs of sections are removed and held together with a flexible adhesive, which also attaches a paper cover to the spine, and the fore edge trimmed flat. Commonly used for paperback books.

case or edition binding
Signatures are sewn together, the spine is flattened, endsheets are applied, and head and tailbands are attached to the spine. Hard covers are attached, and grooves along the cover edge act as hinges.

Canadian
A wiro-bound publication with a wrap-around cover and an enclosed spine. A complete wrap-around cover is a full Canadian and a partial wrap-around is a half Canadian.

saddle stitch
Signatures are nested and bound with wire stitches, applied through the spine along the centerfold.

bookbinding and adding value

Bookbinding involves a variety of processes to produce a finished book. The quality of the materials used and detailing can add value to a design, often in subtle ways, by making the experience of using the book richer and more interesting.

The various sections that form the book block are either stitched or glued to hold them together. The book block may then be shaped or curved. Hardcover books use end papers of stronger stock to provide material for the cover to adhere to, and headbands and tailbands may be added to provide protection to the top and bottom of the binding, as well as provide decorative effect.

A hardcover book provides a designer with many opportunities to be creative. The covering of the hard cover could be leather, velour, linen or another material, it could be screen printed or foil block stamped, the end papers can carry a design, the color of the head and tail bands, and the inclusion of a page marker ribbon for instance.

Certain binding techniques can also help pace a publication through the way that they divide the book block, such as by using a z bind.

ribbon

A ribbon may be attached to the headband to use as a page marker. Pictured right is a hard cover book created by Studio Thompson that features a gold page marker ribbon that creates a classic combination with the red cover and gold foil block.

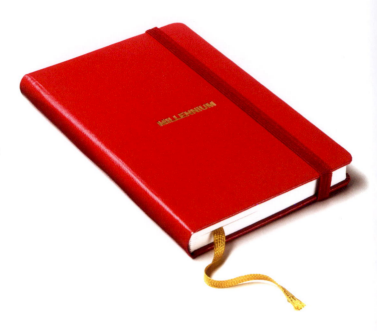

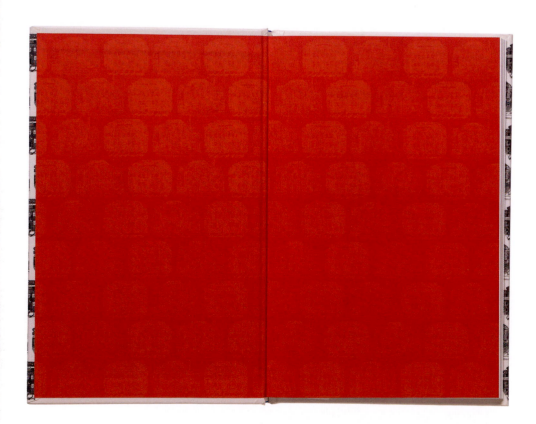

end pages

End pages are the pages that secure the text block to the boards of the cover. They are often not given enough consideration and left blank, but they are a blank canvass with which designers can add a visual element to give a special touch to a publication, hidden just inside its covers. They are typically made from a strong stock such as cartridge paper.

Antique Collectors' Club

Pictured are end papers created by Webb & Webb for one of the many books for the Antique Collectors' Club that always feature creative use of the endpapers. This serves to add interest to individual books, as well as creating a sense of cohesion to the overall series.

16 WYNDHAM PLACE
LONDON W1

Marketing brochure
A Swiss-bound brochure, created by Phage for property developer Studioloop's Wyndham Place in London. The publication uses a color palette of dove grays and golds, and the use of textured stocks and cover materials that reference colors and finishes used throughout the property.

swiss bind
Swiss binding is a soft cover binding method whereby the back cover is mounted and then wrapped over the front, leaving the spine exposed when the cover is open. The book block is sown and its spine can be left exposed or be covered with material such as fabric prior to the application of the book cover. In addition to adding strength and durability to the publication, this method gives an elegant finish that gives designers another element to be creative with.

z-bind
A z-bind features a z-shaped cover that is used to join two separate text blocks, typically with both sections having a perfect bind. This provides a clear yet functional way of separating different types of content, such as different language versions of the same text, or the main information from the appendices, and so on. However, with large publications, this can become unwieldy if the cover stock is not sufficiently robust to support the weight of the pages.

Orange (right)
This publication, produced by Thirteen for the pension plan of mobile telecommunications company, Orange, features a z-bind to separate the two distinct information elements it contains.

case study:

Amado by Hyatt
Anagrama, Mexico

Mexican design agency Anagrama was tasked with creating a visual identity and branding for "Amado" by Hyatt, a Mexican artisan bakery and candy boutique specializing in regional products for Hyatt Hotel lobbies.

The challenge included producing designs for over ten different packaging elements that were separate but coherent and consistent. "Fourteen designs for packaging were printed, but the design was created to be flexible and dynamic for applications in the present and the future," says creative director Mike Herrera.

The branding proposal takes the two iconic Mexican minds—poet Amado Nervo and architect Luis Barragán—to create a visual solution that takes the fine art of traditional artisan bakery to a new contrasting level of modernism. Amado by Hyatt strives to bring together both the romantic and classic spirits of Amado Nervo's poetry and the modernist style of Mexican architect Luis Barragán.

"The project had to be Mexican, premium and modern," says creative director Mike, which meant giving a wide berth to typical Mexican clichés. "We wanted to get away from the typical artisanal souvenirs made en masse and all association to these references. It is very difficult to extract any idea that have not been over-exploited visually, such as pre-Hispanic culture, bandoleros and sugar skulls.

Packaging elements (facing page)
Pictured are packaging elements and details created by Anagrama for Amado by Hyatt that feature gold foil-blocking that help create a contrast between materials and color.

"The finishing touches give contrasts of material and color that play with the light, given that not all the materials have the same reflection"

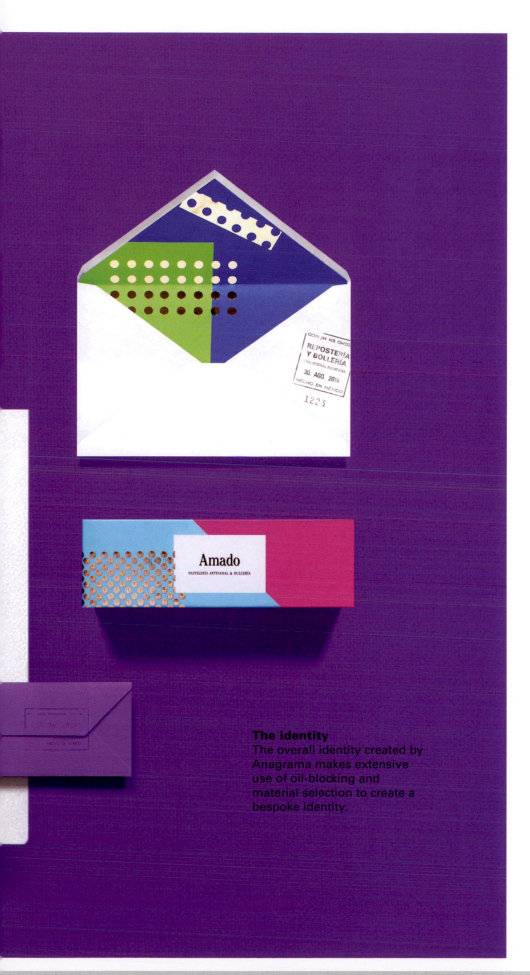

The identity
The overall identity created by Anagrama makes extensive use of oil-blocking and material selection to create a bespoke identity.

Anagrama opted instead for a contemporary innovative solution based on a vivid color palette appropriated from the acid colors and monolithic simplicity of the work of architect Luis Barragán. The packaging presents magenta, yellow and blue hues in simple and geometric forms that mimic the play of light and shadow, and which are refined with spontaneous accents of varnish and foil blocking. "The finishing touches give contrasts of material and color that play with the light, given that not all the materials have the same reflection. It is something that you have to see and touch to understand, that is, you have to pay special attention to the printed material," says Herrera.

The print specification included the use of six Pantone spot colors and a gold foil emboss for some of the packaging materials. Once the design was completed, one of the important challenges was finding a printer with the capacity to produce the packaging to the desired results. "We found a printer that understood us and we achieved an incredible execution. The collaboration between design agency and printer is so important," he says.

appendix

More often than not, print production entails working with standard paper sizes and formats. This appendix provides details of the main standard paper sizes and book formats used internationally. It also includes information about the main standard screen sizes, given that many design jobs often include a digital version in addition to a print version.

MEDLEM
AF
KUNSTNER-
SAMFUNDET

ARKITEKTER OG
BILLEDEKUNSTNERE

Grafisk design: Designbolaget, tryk: Clausen Offset

Akademiraadets og Kunstnersamfundets Jury
Kongens Nytorv 1, 2.sal tv. i porten
1050 København K
Telefon: 33744910
info@akademiraadet.dk
www.akademiraadet.dk

Udgivet i forbindelse med Kunstnersamfundets Dag
december 2010.

Kunstnersamfundet
Pictured is an information folder created by Designbolaget for Kunstnersamfundet
(The Danish Artist Society) that uses different folds and colors to create levels
within it. The different color stocks clearly separate and highlight different types
of information. The colored section in the middle folds out to reveal a map of the
society's structure.

KUNSTNERSAMFUNDET

Kunstnersamfundet er et tværfagligt forum for diskussionen og samspillet mellem arkitektur og billedkunst. Det er et historisk fællesskab mellem skabere af den bundne og den frie kunst.

Som medlem af Kunstnersamfundet får du adgang til at deltage i Akademiets arbejde, som bl.a. er at rådgive staten i kunstneriske anliggender. Du kan på den måde være med til at påvirke kunstens aktuelle situation i Danmark, og du har mulighed for at opnå tillidsposter - ikke kun inden for Akademiets egne rækker, men også udenfor.

Akademiraadet udpeger nemlig blandt Kunstnersamfundets medlemmer repræsentanter eller rådgivere til vigtige og ansvarsfulde poster inden for kunstlivet - såvel offentlige som private organer. Eksempelvis udpeger rådet kunstkonsulenter til Universitets- og Bygningsstyrelsen og kunstnere til repræsentantskaberne i Statens Kunstfond og Kunstråd, Charlottenborg Kunsthal, Den Frie, Det Fynske og Det Jydske Kunstakademi, De Danske Institutter i Rom og Athen, Det særlige Bygningssyn, Statens Værksteder for Kunst og Håndværk samt diverse kunstmuseer og legatbestyrelser.

Et medlemskab af Kunstnersamfundet er derfor den direkte vej for arkitekter og billedkunstnere til at få indflydelse på kunstlivet.

Opbygning af netværk, kollegial bekræftelse, organisationsindsigt, faglige diskussioner, seminarer, konferencer og fester gør det desuden spændende og udviklende at være medlem af Kunstnersamfundet.

SOFIE HESSELHOLDT & VIBEKE MEJLVANG

"Vi har valgt at blive medlemmer af Kunstnersamfundet, da vi begge interesserer os for det fagpolitiske arbejde. Vi håber, at medlemskab af Kunstnersamfundet på sigt vil give større indblik og indflydelse i det kunstpolitiske liv."

"Barrikade", 2008
Plankeværk h. 3 m, sort korsflag.

SØREN LETH

"....efter at have siddet i et udvalg under Akademiraadet stiftede jeg bekendskab med Kunstnersamfundet. Kunstnersamfundets jury opfordrede mig til at søge om optagelse, hvilket jeg gjorde. Primært fordi jeg tænkte, det kunne være en god måde til at udbrede kendskabet til mit arbejde, at udbrede mit netværk i de akademiske kredse og som en slags anerkendelse eller tillidserklæring til mit virke som arkitekt."

The National Museum of Art, Architecture and Design, Oslo, 2010. SLETH MODERNISM.

IVAN ANDERSEN

"Jeg har altid gerne villet være medlem af en loge."

"Tidens Skygge", 2007 Olie og akryl på lærred, 150 cm x 200 cm.

standard sizes

Standardized sizes provide a ready means for selecting product formats that work together, and provide a convenient and efficient means for designers and printers to communicate product specifications and control costs. This spread presents the standard sizes of the US and Canada, and ISO system sizes.

paper and envelope sizes
Standardized sizes provide a ready means for selecting product formats that work together.

US paper standards
The United States, Mexico and Canada use a different set of standard sizes to the rest of the world. The most common sizes in current use are listed to the right. Other sizes are available and are too many to list here, but they are readily available online.

It is also important to note that publication and trim sizes are stated width x height in the US.

The closest match between standard North American and ISO paper sizes are:
Letter (216 x 279 mm), approximate to A4,
Legal (216 x 356 mm) approximate to A4,
Executive (190 x 254 mm) approximate to B5,
Ledger/Tabloid (279 x 432 mm) approximate to A3.

North American paper sizes
Shown below are the main US paper sizes. These were calculated using inches.

Format	[mm w x h]	[in w x h]
Letter	216 × 279	8.5 × 11
Government Letter	203 × 267	8.0 × 10.5
Legal	216 × 356	8.5 × 14
Junior Legal	203 × 127	8.0 × 5.0
Ledger	279 × 431	11 × 17
Tabloid	431 × 279	17 × 11

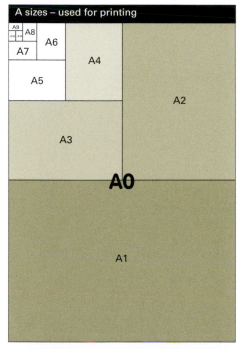

A sizes – used for printing

A9, A10, A8, A7, A6, A5, A4, A3, A2, A1, A0

B sizes – used for books

B9, B10, B8, B7, B6, B5, B4, B3, B2, B1, B0

C sizes – used for envelopes

C9, C10, C8, C7, C6, C5, C4, C3, C2, C1, C0, DL

Format	[mm w x h]	[in w x h]
A0	841 x 1189	33.11 x 46.81
A1	594 x 841	23.39 x 33.11
A2	420 x 594	16.54 x 23.39
A3	297 x 420	11.69 x 16.54
A4	210 x 297	8.27 x 11.69
A5	148 x 210	5.83 x 8.27
A6	105 x 148	4.13 x 5.83
A7	74 x 105	2.91 x 4.13
A8	52 x 74	2.05 x 2.91
A9	37 x 52	1.46 x 2.05
A10	26 x 37	1.02 x 1.46

Format	[mm w x h]	[in w x h]
B0	1000 x 1414	39.37 x 55.67
B1	707 x 1000	27.83 x 39.37
B2	500 x 707	19.69 x 27.83
B3	353 x 500	13.90 x 19.69
B4	250 x 353	9.84 x 13.90
B5	176 x 250	6.93 x 9.84
B6	125 x 176	4.92 x 6.93
B7	88 x 125	3.46 x 4.92
B8	62 x 88	2.44 x 3.46
B9	44 x 62	1.73 x 2.44
B10	31 x 44	1.22 x 1.73

Format	[mm w x h]	[in w x h]
C0	917 x 1297	36.1 x 51.1
C1	648 x 917	25.5 x 36.1
C2	458 x 648	18.03 x 25.51
C3	324 x 458	12.8 x 18.03
C4	229 x 324	9.02 x 12.8
C5	162 x 229	6.38 x 9.02
C6	114 x 162	4.49 x 6.38
C7	81 x 114	3.19 x 4.49
C8	57 x 81	2.24 x 3.19
C9	40 x 57	1.57 x 2.24
C10	28 x 40	1.10 x 1.57
DL	99 x 210	3.7 x 8.3

ISO

Throughout the rest of the world, the ISO standard provides for a range of complementary paper sizes in order to cater for most common printing needs, as shown in the tables above. Generally speaking, A sizes are used for printing everything from posters and technical drawings to magazines, office paper, notepads and postcards; B sizes are used for printing books; while C sizes are used for envelopes that will hold the A sizes.

DL

The DL envelope allows an A4 sheet with two horizontal, parallel folds to fit comfortably inside. This and the DL compliment slip are the same width as an A4 sheet of paper.

Standard stationery formats

The standard for business cards is the ID-1 format of 85.60mm x 53.98mm (3.370 in x 2.125 in). Another popular business card format is A8 (52mm x 74mm).

RA and SRA series

These two series of paper sizes are also based on the ISO standard and are sizes used by printers that are slightly larger than the A series to provide for grip, trim and bleed. To produce an A1 (594mm x 841mm) full bleed poster, the design needs to be printed on to an SRA1 (900mm x 640mm) sheet, which is bigger to allow for trimming to the final size.

book and poster sizes

Books and posters are generally produced in standard formats that provide a ready range of different sizes for a designer to choose from.

standard poster sizes

Posters also have standard sizes that make their production much simpler. The A-series poster system is based around a single sheet of 762mm x 508mm. Multiples of this are used to produce the other sizes in the system, such as six-sheet (1,524mm x 1,016mm) (the most widespread outdoor format due to its compact size). Other standard multiples in this system are 12-sheet (1,524mm x 3,048mm), 48-sheet (3,048mm x 6,096mm) (the standard billboard size that gives 200ft2 of presentation space in landscape orientation) and 96-sheet (3,048mm x 12,192mm).

Two other common formats are European (3,048mm x 3,962mm), a square format popular in Europe, but with the same vertical dimension as the 48- and 96-sheet billboards and the Golden square (6,096mm x 6,096mm), a square format, typically illuminated at night, which helps improve viewer attention by breaking the boundary of standard rectangular dimensions and through its sheer scale.

standard A size posters

	mm [w x h]	in [w x h]		
A0000	1682 × 2378	66.2 x 93.6	1 Sheet	
A00	1189 × 1682	46.8 x 66.2	2 Sheet	
A0	841 × 1189	33.11 x 46.81	4 Sheet	Four sheets of Double Crown
A1	594 × 841	23.39 x 33.11	12 Sheet	Three 4-sheets side-by-side
A2	420 × 594	16.54 x 23.39	16 Sheet	Two x two 4-sheet
A3	297 × 420	11.69 x 16.54	32 Sheet	Four x two 4-sheet
A4	210 × 297	8.27 x 11.69	48 Sheet	Six x two 4-sheet
A5	148 × 210	5.83 x 8.27	64 Sheet	Eight x two 4-sheet
A6	105 × 148	4.13 x 5.83	96 Sheet	Twelve x two 4-sheet
A7	74 × 105	2.91 x 4.13		
A8	52 × 74	2.05 x 2.91		
A9	37 × 52	1.46 x 2.05		
A10	26 × 37	1.02 x 1.46		

standard book sizes

Books come in a wide variety of standard sizes, providing a range of different formats to handle different types of pictorial and textural content, as shown in the table below. A book format is determined by the size of the original sheet of paper used to form its pages and the number of times this is folded before trimming. Folio editions are formed from signatures folded once, quarto from signatures folded twice and octavo three times.

As these are based on a standard paper size they are related and represent a mathematical portion of a sheet of paper. Modern book sizes vary greatly, but often have a relationship to these sizes. The book below, for example, has the same height as Imperial 8vo, but is wider.

In the US, publication sizes are given width x height; elsewhere, they are given hight x width.

common UK book sizes

	bound book size	mm [w x h]	in [w x h]
1	Crown Quarto	189 x 246	7 7/16 x 9 11/16
2	Crown Octavo	123 x 186	4 13/16 x 7 5/16
3	Large Crown Quarto	201 x 258	7 7/8 x 10 3/16
4	Large Crown Octavo	129 x 198	5 1/16 x 7 13/16
5	Demy Quarto	219 x 276	8 5/8 x 10 7/8
6	Demy Octavo	138 x 216	5 7/16 x 8 1/2
7	Royal Quarto	237 x 312	9 5/16 x 12 1/4
8	Royal Octavo	129 x 198	5 1/16 x 7 13/16

common US book sizes

	bound book size	mm [w x h]	in [w x h]
1	Folio	300 x 480	12 x 9
2	Quarto	240 x 300	9 1/2 x 12
3	Octavo	150 x 230	6 x 9
4	Duodecimo	121 x 190	5 x 7 3/8
5	Sextodecimo	100 x 170	4 x 6 3/4
6	Octodecimo	100 x 160	4 x 6 1/2
7	Trigesimo	90 x 140	9 x 14
8	Quadragesimo	65 x 100	2 1/2 x 4

Printing on demand

Print on demand (POD) enables books to be produced in very short print runs. POD printers use standard paper sizes to print on and so standard book trim sizes can be printed by POD.

The short run, bespoke nature of POD also means that non-standard size books can be printed.

US POD sizes (in inches)

5 x 8	8 x 8
5.06 x 7.81	8 x 10
5.25 x 8	8.25 x 11
5.5 x 8.5	8.268 x 11.693
83 x 8.27	8.5 x 11
6 x 9	8.5 x 8.5
6.14 x 9.21	
6.69 x 9.61	
7.5 x 9.25	
7.44 x 9.69	
7 x 10	

screen sizes

With the burgeoning market for smartphones and tablets, in addition to traditional computer monitors, designing for a wide range of screen sizes is now a fact of life. People with smartphones have become used to being able to view high resolution images and smooth scrolling. A designer needs to be aware of the screen capabilities and expectations of the potential user, and how this varies demographically, so that a design can be optimised for its target audience.

resolution and pixels

The continual advance and development of technology means designers face the prospect of having to design for a wide range of screen resolutions. The proliferation of apps on tablets and smartphones means that we increasingly access content on the internet but not necessarily via websites. An October 2014 study by marketing agency Tecmark found that in the UK, the average person uses their phone for three hours and sixteen minutes a day. In the US, eMarketer said in April 2014 that adults spend 5 hours 46 minutes a day with digital media. However, designers increasingly have to design for both mobile and monitors.

Website developer site w3schools.com, says that 99% of its visitors have a screen resolution of 1024x768 pixels or higher, but that they have a wide variety of screen resolutions. In addition to different resolutions and aspect ratios, the pixels on different devices are not even consistent as their density—in terms of their size and the amount of space between them —also varies. With so many variables, where to start? A designer should always design for the target audience and therefore for the type of device or screen that they commonly use. Many mobile web users, particularly those under twenty years of age, are likely to be mobile-only and may rarely use a desktop, laptop or tablet to access the web.

It is virtually an impossible task to design a website that will look the same in every browser, platform and screen resolution, and so designers should optimise their designs for the target audience's most common resolution although it may not be easy to pick what is the most common resolution. Are you creating an internal company website that uses big monitors, or something that will be accessed by teenagers on their smartphones?

While grappling with the range of screen resolutions may seem frustrating it is a good idea to take a pragmatic approach. For example, the 1024×768 resolution was the most widely used screen size for some time and may be a good point to start. You can also design for a fluid layout without tables, using percentage widths that expand and contract to fit a viewer's browser setting, or a responsive design solution to achieve much the same result. That could mean you design for a 1024×768 resolution while ensuring that it transforms gracefully onto another setting.

Creating effective designs not only requires an understanding of device resolutions but also about how devices are used. Is it a desktop device or handheld? Is it mainly used in one environment or many? The research you do into the target user and the equipment they have will be invaluable in making design decisions. Most designers create their work on a desktop computer with a monitor that will probably have a pixel density of 72 or 96 dpi. Is this the same as the target device? Designers must factor in the pixel density of the screen of the typical user to ensure that touchable elements match human fingers and that type is readable. To achieve this in practice means that it is crucial to prototype on the target device(s) from an early stage in development so that you can discover design flaws that you may miss on your desktop monitor.

Top desktop, tablet and console screen resolutions in the UK (Feb to Apr 2015)	Top desktop, tablet and console screen resolutions in the US (Feb to Apr 2015)
1366 x 768	1366 x 768
768 x 1024	1920 x 1080
1920 x 1080	1024 x 768
1280 x 800	1280 x 800
1440 x 900	1440 x 900

glossary

Print production features a wealth of specialist vocabulary to describe different processes, attributes and characteristics. A working knowledge of these terms is essential to ensure accurate communication between design professionals, printers, suppliers and clients.

This glossary is intended to define some of the most commonly used terms, including those that are often confused or used inappropriately. An appreciation and understanding of these terms will facilitate a better understanding and articulation of the print-production process.

standard sizes

glossary

index

Absolute measurement
A finite, fixed value, such as a millimeter.

Binding
A process through which the various pages that comprise a printed work are gathered and securely held together to form a publication.

Bitmap
A raster image that is composed of pixels in a grid.

Bounce
A registration problem occurring when non-color areas print adjacent to heavy color areas.

Bounding box
The square around a digital image whose anchors can be pulled to distort the image.

Brightness
How light or dark a color is. Also called value.

Bulk
The width of a book block.

Burn
An image manipulation technique that lightens tones.

Calliper
The thickness or bulk of a stock.

Channels
The stored color information of a digital image.

Clipping paths
Vector lines used to isolate areas of an image.

CMYK
The subtractive primary colors used as process colors in four-color printing.

Color cast
An imbalance in the colors of an image that leaves one dominant.

Color correction
Techniques to optimise colour performance and remove casts.

Color management
A process governing color translation through the different stages of the printing process.

Color scales
Graduated reference cards printed with precise colors to ensure accurate color reproduction when scanning.

Color space
The array of colors that a graphic device can reproduce.

Curves
Adjustable graphs used to define an image's color and tonality.

Depth of field
The distance in front of and beyond a subject that is in focus.

Die cutting
Use of a steel die to decoratively cut away stock.

Digital printing
The printing of small runs with direct output to a digital printer.

Dodge
An image manipulation technique that darkens tones.

Dot gain
The spreading and enlarging of ink dots on the stock during printing.

Dpi
Dots per inch, a measure of print resolution.

Duotones, tritones and quadtones
Tonal images produced from a monotone original and the use of two, three or four color tones.

Duplexing
The bonding of two stocks to form a single substrate with different characteristics each side.

Em
A relative unit of typographical measurement linked to type size.

Embossing and debossing
The use of a steel die to stamp a design into a substrate to produce a decorative raised or indented surface.

En
A relative unit of typographical measurement linked to type size that is equal to half an em.

End pages
Pages that secure the text block to the boards of the cover in a case binding.

Flaps
An extension of a book cover or dust jacket that fold back and into the publication.

Foil
A finishing process applying colored foil to a substrate via a heated die.

Folding
Different methods for turning a printed sheet into a more compact form or signature.

Four-color black
The darkest black produced when all four process colors are overprinted on each other.

Gamut
Every possible color that can be produced with a given set of colorants on a particular device, such as RGB and CMYK.

Gradient
The increasing weight of one or more colors.

Grayscale
A tonal scale of achromatic tones with varying levels of white and black used to convert continuous-tone color photographs into approximate levels of gray.

Half-tone
An image made from half-tone dots, produced by screening a continuous tone image for printing.

Head and tailbands
Protective patterned or colored bands that form part of a book block binding.

Hue
The unique characteristic of a color formed by different wavelengths of light.

Imposition
The sequence and position that pages will print before being cut, folded and trimmed.

Interpolation
One of several computer processes used to regenerate an image after it has been resized.

Laminate
A layer of plastic coating, heat sealed on to a substrate to produce a smooth and impervious finish.

Laser cutting
Use of a laser to cut intricate shapes into a stock.

Layers
Different levels of a digital image that can be worked on separately.

Layout
The management of form and space in a design.

Line art
An image with no tonal variation, fill color or shading that does not require screening for printing.

Masks
A graduated layer or filter that is used to blend different images.

Moiré
An interference pattern caused by poor half-tone screen alignment.

Neutral gray
A color made from 50 per cent cyan, 40 per cent magenta and 40 per cent yellow that allows designers to accurately see color balance by providing a neutral contrast.

Overprinting
Where one ink overprints another so that they mix to create different colors.

Paper grain
The alignment of paper fibers during the manufacturing process.

Parallax
A visual effect that makes an object appear displaced when seen from different viewpoints.

Perforation
Cuts in a substrate that allow parts to be detached or to create a decorative effect.

Pica
An absolute unit of typographical measurement equal to 12pts. There are six picas in an inch.

Pixel
The basic unit of programmable color on a computer display or in a digital image. The physical size of a pixel or picture element depends on the resolution setting.

Point
An absolute unit of typographical measurement. There are 72pts in an inch.

Ppi
Pixels per inch, a measure of screen resolution.

Printing
One of several processes that apply ink or varnish from a plate to a substrate through the application of pressure.

Proofing
Various tests used in the print production process to ensure accurate reproduction.

Raster
A fixed resolution image composed of pixels in a grid.

Recto / verso
The right- and left-hand pages of a spread.

Registration black
A black obtained from 100 per cent coverage of the four process colors (cyan, magenta, yellow and black).

Relative measurement
A value determined in relation to a key reference.

Resolution
The number of pixels contained in a digital image, expressed as ppi.

Reverse out
Where a design is an unprinted area in a solid block of color.

RGB
The additive primary colors of white light.

Rich black
A black that uses a shiner to prevent the bounce registration problem.

Saturation
The purity of a color and the amount of gray it contains. Also called chroma.

Scanning
A process through which an image or piece of artwork is converted into an electronic file.

Shiner
The underprinting of a process color to strengthen a black and prevent registration errors.

Special characters
Typographical symbols that may be required when use of the normal character set causes problems.

Stochastic printing
Use of different dots sizes and random placement to avoid the appearance of moiré patterns.

Stock
The substrate that a job is printed upon.

Text block
The book block of printed signatures or sections of a publication.

Thermography
A print finishing process producing raised lettering by fusing thermographic powder to a design in an oven.

Tint
A color printed at ten per cent increments of a full solid color created using half-tone dots of different sizes.

Varnish
A colorless coating applied to a printed piece to protect and enhance visual appearance.

Vector
A resolution-independent and scalable image defined by mathematical formulae or paths rather than pixels.

Web-safe font
A font that can be displayed by common operating systems such as Windows and Mac OS.

Z-bind
A binding method that holds two blocks in a z-shaped cover.

index

Acknowledgements

We would like to thank all the contributing design studios that generously provided examples of their work for this second edition, with a special mention to those that provided the case studies for their willingness to provide insights into their work and design decision processes. And a final thank you to all the staff at Bloomsbury for their help, patience and support in producing this volume. A special thank you to Sean Brennan, for his work on supplementary materials.